An Outbreak of Peace

Angola's situation of confusion

D1526919

dp davidphilip

First published in 2005 in southern Africa by
David Philip, an imprint of New Africa Books (Pty) Ltd,
99 Garfield Road, Claremont 7700, South Africa
www.newafricabooks.co.za

ISBN 0-86486-676-3
Editor/proofreader: Michael Collins
Layout and design: Charlene Bate
Cover design: Abdul Amien
Printed and bound in the Republic of South Africa by
CTP Book Printers, Cape

Front cover: Calala quartering area, one of 35 such areas where
former UNITA men were to surrender their weapons and assemble
with their families.
Back cover: (right) At the edge of the ocean, Luanda often seemed to
turn its back on the war; (left) peasant farmer at Camacupa, part of a
population of *deslocados* fed by donor agencies.

Contents

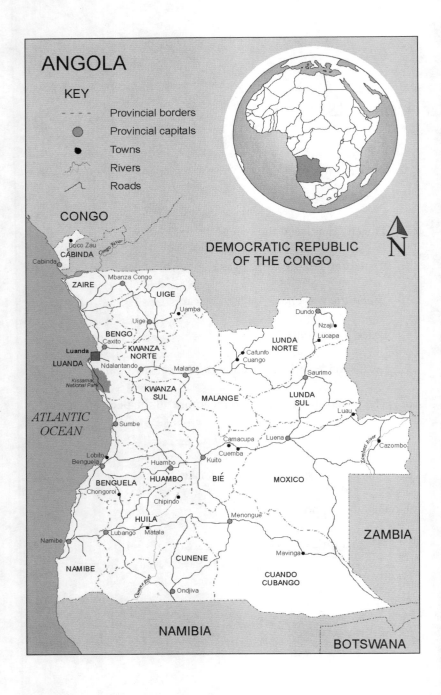

ANGOLA

KEY
- - - - Provincial borders
  ●   Provincial capitals
  ●   Towns
         Rivers
         Roads

CONGO

CABINDA
Buco Zau
Cabinda

DEMOCRATIC REPUBLIC
OF THE CONGO

N

ZAIRE
Mbanza Congo

UIGE
Uamba
Uige

BENGO
Caxito

Luanda
LUANDA

KWANZA
NORTE
Ndalantando   Malange

Kissama
National Park

Dundo
Nzaji
Lucapa

LUNDA
NORTE
Cafunfo
Cuango

Saurimo

ATLANTIC
OCEAN

KWANZA
SUL
Sumbe

MALANGE

LUNDA
SUL
Luau

Lobito
Benguela
Huambo

BENGUELA
Chongoroi

HUAMBO

Chipindo

Camacupa   Luena
Cuemba
Kuito

BIÉ

MOXICO

Cazombo

Zambeze River

Namibe

HUILA
Lubango Matala

Menongue

ZAMBIA

NAMIBE

CUNENE

Mavinga

Cunene River
Ondjiva

CUANDO
CUBANGO

NAMIBIA

BOTSWANA

Acknowledgements

Even before I ever thought of writing a book, living in Angola for two years and attempting to understand the place would have been impossible without the help of many people both in and outside of the country. Anabela and Sebastião Brandão provided me with a home during my first months in Angola. Rafael Marques and Fern Teodoro have been a constant source of wisdom, advice and support ever since that first trip to the Mausoleum. Margrit Coppé and Fergus Power helped keep me sane while in Angola, and their interest and belief in this book, even when it was no more than an idea, has more than anything else helped keep me writing and editing. In that task I have also enjoyed the support of numerous other friends in Angola, South Africa and the UK.

Colin Murphy unearthed the newspaper clipping that revealed how deliberately the Angolan government had set about emptying the countryside of its farmers in the pursuit of Jonas Savimbi. Zoé Eisenstein helped me keep my sense of humour (almost) until the end. Alejandro Mena gave me a place to do much of the writing of the first chapters – as did Stefaans Brümmer and Karen Schoonbee, later on.

My thanks are due to all the Angolan journalists, braver souls than I will ever need to be, who patiently shared their insights – João van Dunem, Walter dos Santos, Gilberto Neto, Tomás de Melo, João Pinto, Alves Fernandes, Siona Casimiro, Manuel Mwanza, Herculano Coroado (wherever you may be now) – not to mention the *estrangeiras* who were there before me: Lara Pawson and Anita Coulson.

To all those organisations that offered me flights, lifts and accommodation I am grateful, especially since my fascination with unravelling the history of the last years of the war often had little in common with their own public relations agenda: Acción Contra el Hambre, Concern, GOAL, the International Committee of the Red Cross, Médecins sans Frontières, the Open Society Initiative for Southern Africa, Oxfam, the UN Office for the Co-ordination of Humanitarian Affairs (OCHA) and the World Food Programme (WFP). In particular, I am indebted to Marcelo Spina Hering of WFP and Julie Thompson of OCHA whose own stressful workload never prevented them from being obliging providers of information. Maria Flynn's hospitality whenever I visited Uige was memorable.

And to the diplomat who invented the concept of peace breaking out – you wished to remain anonymous, but you know who you are, and I valued our conversations more than just for the fact that they yielded the title of this book.

Introduction

Thirteen kilometres from the centre of Luanda, the city straggles to an end. The slums finally left behind, the road sticks for a while to a straight stretch of coastline, where the last few pastel-coloured, balustraded concrete villas line the beach, as close as they dare lest they be swallowed in the iron-coloured mud. Then the road loses the shore for a while, climbing the ridge that separates this bay from the next, until a bend at the crest of the hill opens up a new vista.

Across the mudflats rises a small headland, topped by a little whitewashed building glowing stark against the ocean that comes close to surrounding it. Here, on the cusp of the land and the sea, is the earliest knot in the net that ties Angola to the world beyond the horizon. From up on the hill, you might take it for a chapel. In fact, it was a prison, a transit point for some of the estimated two million slaves who left Angola between the 16th and the 19th century – the last they would see of the country before they sank with the sun over the horizon in the direction of Brazil or the Caribbean.

Portuguese seamen first landed in Angola in the last decade of the 15th century. Portugal was and is a coast-hugging nation, a nation that, trapped between Spain and the Atlantic, turned to the ocean to find its place in history. As in Europe, so in the colonies. It would be nearly 400 years before Portuguese settlers in Angola showed any inclination to move into the interior, by which time the Atlantic slave trade had come to an end. In the meantime, the trade could not have happened without the participation of African intermediaries.

The historian Patrick Chabal argues:

> The effects of the slave trade on inland African communities varied enormously, between those which raided and traded slaves and those which were raided. It was Africans who sold the slaves to the traders acting as intermediaries for the Luanda Creole merchants. This Creole community lived in some considerable separation from the interior, turned as it was towards the Brazilian and Portuguese societies of which it felt a part – and with which indeed it had complex family, social and economic links. It is clear, therefore, that most inland Africans would, long before the colonial period, have viewed these city-based Creoles as quite alien.[1]

African participation in the slave trade was by no means unique to Angola. Nor were the rifts that slavery hammered between two classes of indigenous people. How, then, did Angola differ from Senegal or Ghana or any other African territory where the earliest colonial contact was defined by slavery?

Defenders of Portuguese colonial policy often start by assuming a particularly close interaction between colonists and colonised. The Portuguese colonies are portrayed as a place where intermarriage was nothing unusual, and where the mere fact of skin pigment was held less important than speaking Portuguese and accepting the rest of the cultural baggage that goes along with the shushing consonants and nasal vowels. An African in the Portuguese colonies could, in theory, become an *assimilado*: one who has been assimilated. The goal of assimilation was to cease to be African in all but colour. In this way, the Portuguese style of colonisation has been seen as a virtue rather than a peculiarity. The Brazilian writer Gilberto Freyre provided it with theoretical respectability under the name 'lusotropicalism', arguing that it produced a harmonious hybrid society of black, brown and white.

Far more compelling, however, are the arguments that lusotropicalism was nothing more than a ruse to justify the colonial

---

[1] Chabal et al: *A History of Postcolonial Lusophone Africa*. London, Hurst and Co, 2002. p 108.

presence in territories where race relations were no more egalitarian than they were in the French or British colonies. 'To most non-Portuguese, lusotropicalism is a romantic myth (at best) or an invidious lie (at worst) used to obscure the realities of Portuguese colonialism,' wrote the American historian Gerald Bender, in the opening chapter of a book that systematically demolishes the idea that Portuguese colonialism – in Angola, at any rate – was based on anything other than European supremacism.

Bender's book *Angola Under the Portuguese* showed that the lusotropicalist vision had no prospect of ever becoming a reality in a territory as large and diverse as Angola. As a theory, moreover, its effect was insidious. Far from creating a society of equal opportunity, the possibility of cultural assimilation – when offered to some and not to others – both ran parallel to and deepened the divisions caused by the slave trade. Today, the strata of Angolan society – reduced to the simplest terms – include *mestiços*, Old Creole families (the descendants of the black elite which flourished following the first colonial contact), Portuguese-speaking blacks on the coast, Portuguese-speaking blacks in the interior towns, and the *camponeses* (peasants) who speak indigenous languages.

It is such divisions that enable some *mestiço* (mixed race) Angolans to talk of 'the blacks' with a contempt comparable to that engendered by apartheid. It is what allowed Jonas Savimbi, as he engaged the Luanda government in conflict for a quarter of a century, to talk of coastal Angola and all it represented as being the fiefdom of the whites and their *mestiço* kin. And more recently – in the first years of the 21st century – it meant that the coastal rulers could sleep easily after sending in the troops to conduct *limpeza*: cleaning out every peasant farmer in the east of the country in the name of winning peace.

Those eastern reaches became part of Angola only after the Berlin Conference of 1885, the power-drunk plan devised by King Leopold II of the Belgians to section Africa among the nation states of Europe, with Britain and France the main beneficiaries. The conference ruled that colonial sovereignty would be bestowed only upon those countries that occupied the territory they had staked out. Needing to consolidate its claims, Portugal began extending its administration into the interior.[2] Over half a century later, while Britain and France prepared to pull out of their colonies, the Portuguese continued to flood into theirs. Far from contemplating independence, the Portuguese government declared in 1951 that its African territories would henceforth cease to be colonies and be treated instead as overseas provinces of Portugal.

The presence of liberation movements and, later, independent governments elsewhere in Africa gave moral and material support to the emergence of independence movements in Angola from the late 1950s and into the 1960s. Inside the country, though, there was nothing to give a sense of common purpose to the movements that emerged in distinct regions of Angola, divided by history as well as by the country's sprawling geography, as they pursued their own visions of an independent state.[3]

One movement grew up among the ethnic Bakongo exiles in the newly independent Zaire: people who had been driven out of Angola when Portuguese settler farmers had moved into the area. Betraying its origins in the name of União das Populações do Norte de Angola (UPNA – Northern Angolan People's Union), it later dropped the 'Northern' and, in 1962, became the Frente Nacional da Libertação de Angola (FNLA). Its leader, Holden Roberto, was both a disciple of Frantz Fanon and a friend and brother-in-law of Mobutu Sese Seko.

A second movement emerged in the early 1960s among the *assimilado*, *mestiço* and white populations of the coast and the ethnic Kimbundu of Luanda's hinterland. Multi-ethnic in character, the Movimento Popular da Libertação de Angola (MPLA) professed an ideology of non-racialism and non-tribalism. Photographs of its leadership in the early 1970s show a group of people who, on average, are surprisingly light-skinned for a tropical African liberation movement. This was the group of Angolans with the closest cultural

---

[2] Fernando Andreson Guimarães, *The Origins of the Angolan Civil War.* p 3.

[3] Guimarães, and David Birmingham's chapter, 'Angola' in Patrick Chabal et al *A History of Postcolonial Lusophone Africa*, provide the fullest and most objective analyses of the emergence of the liberation movements and the rivalries between them.

ties to Portugal; an important part of its early constituency comprised exiles in Europe and students at Portugal's universities who had exchanged ideas with the Salazar regime's socialist opponents. The third movement started out in 1966 as a breakaway from the FNLA. Jonas Savimbi (who had become foreign minister in the government in exile established by Holden Roberto) originated a long way from Holden's northern heartland: he was a son of the Planalto Central (Central Plateau), the cool and fertile highlands of south-central Angola. In the beginning, Savimbi's political skill lay in his ability to mobilise the peasant farmers of this area, who, like Savimbi himself, were of Angola's majority Ovimbundu ethnic group. Savimbi resigned his government-in-exile post in 1964 and, two years later, established UNITA, taking his Ovimbundu supporters with him.

This book does not set out to analyse or to judge Savimbi's impact on what happened over the three ensuing decades. Suffice to say that even commentators who would normally hesitate to ascribe historical developments to the actions and personality of an individual concede that without Savimbi, Angolan history would have looked different. While Savimbi may have been lauded in the West – notably by Ronald Reagan – as a champion of anti-communist interests, he succeeded in convincing Angolan peasants that only he could save them from the whites and *mestiços* down on the coast and the Cubans from across the sea; that only he could allow them to be proud black Africans. Recurring allegations that Savimbi dabbled in the supernatural helped to sustain the mystique. Even at the time of Savimbi's death in 2002, a journalist from the state-controlled media who viewed the body could not resist concluding that pieces of cloth twisted around the dead man's wrist were a sign of his participation in witchcraft.

By the time I was born, in South Africa in 1967, the first cycle of decolonisation in Africa was complete. Starting with Ghana, 10 years earlier, the British and French colonies to the north of the Zambezi had become independent. In southern Africa, however, white people remained in charge, as far north as the Congo River in the west and the Rovuma River in the east, with the exception of three enclaves: sparsely-populated Botswana, and tiny Lesotho and Swaziland. In South Africa, white control was codified in a system called apartheid whose most vigorous exponent, Hendrik Verwoerd, had been assassinated a year earlier. In Rhodesia, 1965 had seen the Unilateral Declaration of Independence, when white Rhodesians installed their own apartheid-style state. In Angola and Mozambique, meanwhile, Portugal showed no signs of budging. Thanks to South Africa's de facto annexation of South West Africa, apartheid extended all the way to the border of Angola.

A coup by pro-democracy army officers in Portugal in April 1974 changed the political landscape in Angola almost overnight. The new regime in Lisbon wanted to end the colonial wars that were consuming half of Portugal's public spending, and announced its willingness to concede sovereignty to 'the Angolan people'. A prospective transitional power-sharing agreement between the three liberation movements soon broke down, as each of the three aimed for absolute power.

The real differences of perspective between the three rival movements were fuelled by the fact that the Cold War superpowers gave their backing to opposing factions. The United States had at first encouraged the FNLA, but later turned its attention to UNITA. Ironically enough for a movement that espoused a black nationalist ideology, UNITA had already begun to accept help from apartheid South Africa.

No less ironic was the decision by the MPLA, led by relatively well-off urban dwellers, to espouse socialism and eventually to accept help from Cuba: a decision that flowed from the movement's socialist intellectual tradition and its links with the left-wing opposition to the Salazar dictatorship. Although the MPLA had sought a non-aligned position in relation to the Cold War, suspicion of its motives prompted South Africa and the United States to shun the MPLA and actively to support its opponents. The MPLA looked to Cuba for help – and any hope of resolving Angola's internal tensions disappeared as the country became a Cold War battlefield.

When Portugal withdrew its last forces on 11 November 1975, the MPLA held little more than Luanda. Helped by Cuban soldiers, military advisors and arms, the MPLA routed the FNLA forces that were approaching Luanda from the north, and halted the advance of the South Africans from the south. UNITA, which initially established a rival capital in the central Angolan city of Huambo, was pushed back to the far south-east of the country, where it re-armed itself with South African support. Throughout the 1980s, UNITA guerrillas continued to destabilise the MPLA regime, backed by the South African Defence Force which made frequent incursions into the south of the country.

It was through these military adventures that Angola first began to enter our consciousness in South Africa. National service on 'the border' became a fact of life for most white South African men who came of age in the late 1970s and the 1980s. Talk of the 'border' helped to obscure the fact that the army was being deployed not on the border of South Africa, but South African-occupied Namibia's border with Angola – and frequently, still further north.

Browsing in a second-hand bookshop during the writing of this book, I came upon a volume that gives a good idea of what many white South Africans were thinking at the time. *Adeus Angola* is a memoir by Willem Steenkamp, a South African journalist who was later defence correspondent of the *Cape Times*, and who went into Angola as a soldier. His book is a sometimes critical but generally positive assessment of South Africa's military presence there. In the end Steenkamp rejects – with contempt – the suggestion that the South African invasion prolonged the conflict in Angola by forcing the MPLA to turn to Cuba for help and ruled out the possibility of detente between the governments of John Vorster and Agostinho Neto:

> Judged in the knowledge of previous communist takeovers in other countries, it is clear that the MPLA's course of action went according to a carefully-planned scenario, of which the flow of arms and men from the communist bloc was an integral part.

It was a simple, straightforward communist land-grab, and whereas the South African intervention might have necessitated a somewhat greater intervention than had been budgeted for, the outside aid would have been furnished in any case.

Though Steenkamp takes the view that the MPLA functioned as the stooges of an international communist strategy, he acknowledges that 'Neto's movement had less of a tribal bias than the other two' and treats UNITA with a journalist's scepticism. Other, less reasoned, accounts of the war paint Savimbi's UNITA as the messiah of the Angolan peasantry against the ubiquitous 'communist forces'. A recent internet search drew up an article written in June 2004 by the right-wing Christian missionary Peter Hammond who had been working in UNITA-held territory in 1986 when he heard, over the BBC, American president Ronald Reagan's promise of anti-aircraft missiles to UNITA. Hammond writes:

> Not long afterwards the Stinger missiles began to arrive in UNITA controlled Free Angola. Soviet aircraft were shot down. The bombing and strafing of villagers, schools and churches came to an end. Without any doubt, Ronald Reagan's policies saved many thousands of lives in Angola.[4]

The contrary view of events received little expression in South Africa at the time, but was embraced and made concrete by a number of European writers who sympathised with an MPLA whose intellectual heritage owed much to a European socialist tradition. For these observers, the MPLA represented a fresh start in the decolonisation of Africa: the opportunity to make a break from a first wave of decolonisation that had already produced despots such as Mobutu Sese Seko, in the pay of the West.

In his account of the weeks surrounding Angolan independence in 1975, titled *Another Day of Life*, Polish correspondent Ryszard Kapuscinski recalls how he telexed his news editor from Luanda: 'It is more or less clear what will happen, which is that the Angolans will win.' By 'the Angolans' he meant the MPLA. Basil Davidson,

---

4 http://www.frontline.org.za/articles/reagan.htm

who spent time in the bush with MPLA guerrillas in the 1960s, managed to write a book called *In the Eye of the Storm: Angola's People* with barely a mention of either the FNLA or UNITA.

For us in South Africa, and indeed those in much of the English-speaking world, these were the two mirror-image good-guy-bad-guy pictures of Angola that were presented. It was impossible for outsiders to conceive of Angola without choosing sides – not on the basis of any previous knowledge of Angolan realities, but on where we stood in relation to the Cold War or the dichotomy between South Africa's apartheid present and prospective non-racial and (so we believed at the time) socialist future.

Growing up in white South Africa, it was almost inevitable that my own first information about Angola would be based on the premise that Savimbi, our man, was the one saving Angola – and the rest of southern Africa – from the communist invaders. The perspectives available to me broadened when I began studying at the University of Cape Town, a place where criticism of the government was close to orthodoxy, the more so when the South African state started, through the second half of the 1980s, to uproot the rule of law and adopt increasingly violent measures against its opponents at home and abroad. I recall holding placards denouncing yet another SADF incursion into Angola, photocopying pamphlets in support of conscientious objectors – and I extended my studies long enough to avoid being conscripted.

However profound the differences in outlook between the MPLA and UNITA – differences that pre-existed the Cold War division – it was the encouragement and material support of the rival superpowers that allowed the war between them to continue almost without a pause for nearly 15 years after independence. In the early 1990s, therefore, it was taken as given that the detente on the international political stage would have its payoff in Angola, as it did in Namibia, South Africa, and Eastern Europe. Soviet and US government representatives, meeting in Namibia for that country's independence in March 1990, agreed on terms for the conclusion of the war in Angola.[5] The following year, the MPLA and UNITA entered talks in the Portuguese seaside town of Bicesse. They agreed to a ceasefire, followed by a process of disarmament that would be supervised by the UN and create the conditions for multi-party elections, again under international supervision.[6]

Between the signing of the Bicesse accord in May 1991 and the elections of September 1992, Angola enjoyed an interlude of peace and unqualified optimism seen neither before nor since. 'It was the only time that you could get oranges in Luanda,' an Angolan friend recalled a decade later. People started moving around the country again, and the capital on its arid coastline briefly enjoyed the produce of the highlands rather than looking to overseas imports. What became clear later was that UNITA had agreed to the Bicesse plan only because it felt assured of electoral victory.

As the elections drew nearer, UNITA lagged behind the schedule for disarmament. The MPLA enjoyed access to the state media and all the other advantages of incumbency in running its campaign. Voting went ahead peacefully, but as vote counting proceeded and the MPLA edged ahead, Savimbi dropped increasingly strong hints that he would not accept the election results. When the electoral commission announced a narrow victory to the MPLA and to President José Eduardo dos Santos, UNITA went back to war, surprising an MPLA whose army, unlike UNITA, had largely complied with the disarmament agreement.

Within months, the rebels had seized control of much of the interior of the country. A nation that had been expecting peace now found itself thrust into the midst of the worst fighting Angola had ever seen as UNITA and the MPLA battled for control of the main cities of the interior. During this period, the main street of Kuito, capital of Bié province and one of the main cities of the Central

---

[5] See David Birmingham's chapter, 'Angola' in Patrick Chabal et al, *A History of Postcolonial Lusophone Africa*. p 170.

[6] Karl Maier *(Angola: Promises and Lies)* and Judith Matloff *(Fragments of a Forgotten War)* have provided vivid accounts of the period from the Bicesse accords through the resumption of armed conflict in the 1990s.

Plateau, became a frontline for nine months, half the town becoming a government-controlled enclave cut off from surrounding farmlands and from the wider world. UNITA, meanwhile, held the city of Huambo, capital of the province of the same name, for 55 days until government forces battled their way up from the coast.

The MPLA-led government used its considerable oil wealth to re-arm and remobilise. Once again, it enlisted help from abroad, not from Cuba now, but from its old enemy, South Africa. White soldiers recently retired from the South African Defence Force, many of whom had once fought against the MPLA, were now engaged as mercenaries against UNITA. The rebels, meanwhile, may have lost the support of their former allies in Washington and Pretoria, but funded their war effort through control of many of Angola's alluvial diamond fields. The Lusaka peace accord of 1994 attempted to commit both sides to a cessation of hostilities, but the agreement broke down amid mutual recriminations.[7]

International awareness of the role played by diamonds in funding both UNITA and the Revolutionary United Front rebel movement in Sierra Leone prompted sanctions against 'conflict diamonds' in the late 1990s; these measures, although never completely effective, certainly left UNITA in a more and more fragile position. The ousting of UNITA's old ally, Mobutu Sese Seko, in Zaire in 1997, was a further blow. Yet, in 1998, when the government lost patience with the stop-start progress and resolved to defeat UNITA by force of arms, the rebels were still able to put up a fight.

'Christmas '98 – the worst Christmas ever,' I was told by one Angolan journalist who had got his stories by hitching rides on the military transport planes when UNITA started shelling provincial capitals in 1998. 'When we took off from the airports in the provinces,' he said, 'women were throwing their babies onto the planes saying "Please take my baby". They thought it was going to be

---

[7] See Human Rights Watch: *Angola Unravels: The Rise and Fall of the Lusaka Peace Process.*

a repeat of 1993. They had lived through so much. One time we rode back with 80 corpses. We were sitting on top of them.'

Not only did the return to war throw ordinary Angolans into a daily round of killing, hunger, rape and homelessness that surpassed anything seen in the war's earlier stages, it also extinguished the hopes of a democratic future that had accompanied the elections. Under the smokescreen of war, the constitution was sidelined in a way that helped to concentrate power in the hands of José Eduardo dos Santos – president since Neto's death in 1979 – who was now accountable neither to the ruling party of his old Marxist-Leninist days nor to the parliament that had been elected in 1992. The mandate of both the parliament and the administration expired in 1997, but the war provided an excuse for avoiding further elections.

The lack of accountability in government was nowhere more evident than in the management of the country's oil revenues, a state of affairs that left billions of dollars unaccounted for, and presumed stolen by powerful individuals within the government. Influential figures in government and in the army also profited directly from the war, with generals helping themselves to diamond concessions or using military planes as a commercial air service.[8]

In 2001 – some 15 years after the South African Defence Force wanted to send me there – I went to Angola for the first time, as a correspondent for the BBC. Shortly before leaving London for Angola I met a journalist from one of the independent papers that had emerged with the promises of press freedom around the time of the 1992 elections, and whose journalists were now finding themselves banned, threatened or imprisoned when they tried to speak out against corruption and the war. In the grinding wind and rain of an English March day, he asked me: 'Is Canada colder than England?' His eyes widened with horror when I answered in the affirmative, but this did not stop him from going on to seek asylum in Canada. His assessment of his own country was: '*Angola não é*

---

[8] Tony Hodges' book *Angola: Anatomy of an Oil State* is the most thorough account to date of the looting of state assets by members of the political elite.

um país. É uma situação. Uma situação de confusão. Angola is not a country. It is a situation. A situation of confusion.

By the turn of the century, the Angolan government had recaptured the last of the administrative centres, and regained control of the most important diamond fields. The nature of the war had changed: it was no longer a battle for control of territory, but UNITA proved highly effective as a mobile guerrilla force, embarrassing the government by striking where it was least expected.

The most audacious of these attacks was on Caxito, a town 'at the gates of Luanda' as one of the independent papers put it, and it is with this incident, a few days before my arrival in Angola, that this narrative begins. Less than a year later, Jonas Savimbi would be dead, and a society where two generations had known nothing but war would be trying to figure out the meaning of peace.

Coming as I do from a country where, consciously or unconsciously, we have always tried to reduce and define Angola in the terms of our own conflicts, I was soon to realise the complete inadequacy of either of the versions of history that I knew, as a way of accounting for what I saw and heard. UNITA was not a creation of PW Botha and Ronald Reagan, but neither was Savimbi the saviour of the black Angolan peasantry. The MPLA was not the vanguard in a proposed Soviet takeover of Africa, but neither did the 'people's movement' with its anti-imperialist vision for Africa seem much better than the Mobutus and the Bothas it had once sought to oppose. Rather than either movement representing the Angolan people against the stooges of an external aggressor, the very idea of 'the people' was contested. The very notion of what it meant to be Angolan was at stake.

More recently, Angolans have been told that they will have the chance to vote in the second half of 2006, 13 years after the first and last elections. Although peace has been the necessary condition for the next election to happen, Angolan politics remain forged in a furnace of war. Most Angolans will be voting for one or other of the parties that, for 25 years, denied them peace. After so many years during which political identity was a product of military control, it looks likely that the election, and the one that follows, could simply endorse the balance of forces as it was at the war's end.

As an account of Angola, this book can only be partial and subjective. As much as being about Angola, however, it is about a foreigner, *um estrangeiro*, in Angola trying to unpick the contradictory accounts of the past and to make sense of a situation sown with the seeds of confusion and distress. If I succeed in persuading others to do the same, then writing this book will have been worthwhile.

Justin Pearce
Johannesburg, May 2005

1

The city that faced the sea

An artificial leg was all that had saved Isaura Maionga from being abducted. Or so the teenager believed. She had watched soldiers take away 60 of her fellow pupils from the school hostel in Caxito on the night of Friday 4 May 2001. A week later, dressed in jeans and a white T-shirt worthy of an Omo ad, her hair tightly braided with nylon extensions, Isaura told her story with a troubling lack of emotion. At that point she did not know whether her schoolmates were alive or not.

UNITA's men had arrived while some of the students were still up and about late that night. 'I saw men in uniforms, and I thought they were policemen until one of them started shooting in the air. We went into the dormitories, and locked the doors,' she said. 'Then the soldiers started banging on the doors. We opened them – because we were worried we would be shot if we did not.'

The rebels held the children – aged between 10 and 18 – at gunpoint in a yard outside while their comrades ransacked the dormitories and carried off clothes and blankets, before moving on to the food storeroom. There they ordered the older children each to take a 50-kilogram sack of flour or rice. It was at that point, Isaura said, that she showed a soldier her artificial leg and pleaded she would not be able to keep up with them on a march. She could have been shot dead on the spot for this; instead, she was left behind.

'I saw the last people leaving,' she recalled. 'When they were gone, I ran and hid in the bush because I was afraid other soldiers would come.'

The school was situated a little way outside the centre of Caxito, so Isaura did not know at the time that another party of rebels had already rampaged through the town. According to Sister Jovita and Sister Concepción, two Mexican nuns at the mission in the centre of the town, the government forces had not stopped to put up a fight. 'The soldiers and the police ran away. For an hour and a half there was a lot of *confusão* – shooting right outside our house.'

Sister Jovita and Sister Concepción had been in Angola long enough for *confusão* – literally, confusion – to have seeped into their vocabulary. In this case, *confusão* meant the violent death of at least 200 people.

Abductions and massacres were nothing unusual in Angola in 2001, all part of the background hum of news that reached the capital's radios. What was significant about Caxito was that it lies only 60 km from Luanda, which for the best part of a decade had managed to keep the war at a distance. The last time the city had come close to war had been in 1992, nine years earlier, when UNITA, the rebel movement with its roots in the countryside, had lost the elections that followed the 1990 Bicesse peace accord.

There are conflicting accounts of what happened when the electoral commission announced victory to the ruling MPLA party and to President José Eduardo dos Santos. It is known that MPLA supporters went on a killing spree against members of the Ovimbundu ethnic group, who were associated with UNITA. What is better known is that Jonas Savimbi, whose name is synonymous with UNITA, the movement he founded in the 1960s, ordered his troops back to war. UNITA officials and soldiers fled Luanda and had soon taken back most of the country by force, starting with Caxito.

The Mexican nuns had witnessed that attack too ('the Kimbundus fled, the Ovimbundus stayed, but UNITA didn't attack the mission').

The MPLA government had held onto the coast, most importantly to the colonial capital where the party established a government in 1975. From there, it started to fight back. The Angolan army pushed UNITA out of Caxito in 1993. As the army edged forward, the government installed its administrators, one by one, in the towns of the interior until, by the turn of the century, the whole country was under state control.

In theory, at least. *Em princípio*, as Angolans were fond of saying.

The Caxito attack of 2001 had demonstrated how fragile that principle was. The capital's residents no longer enjoyed the comfort of knowing they could travel for a whole hour out of the city limits before putting themselves in any danger.

Luanda looks across the Atlantic, the melancholy hip-sway of its *kizomba* music sounding more Latin American than African. Young women in Luanda wore tight pants and bikini tops, fashions transported straight from Copacabana Beach. Anyone speaking Kimbundu or Umbundu or Kikongo was shunned in shops and government offices that recognised no language other than Portuguese.

The city turned its back on Africa, just as it turned its back on the war. The planes that flew into Luanda from South Africa avoided Angolan territory altogether, taking a straight course across the brown lands of Botswana and Namibia to where the Cunene River reaches the sea and marks the southern border of Angola. Only then did they turn north and follow the beach all the way to Luanda.

Seen from the air, the city seemed to grow slowly out of the sand: first the scrappy edges of the slums, then the blocks of flats of the centre all the same dusty colour. A railway yard with trains rusting into the tracks. A fairground with a Ferris wheel, not moving. Arriving a few days after the Caxito attack, I watched the city appear and disappear as the plane swung out over the bay, which was more like a pool defined by the curve of the coast and a long sandy island. Then we were over the ocean of houses once more, and tilted towards the runway. Before we reached the terminal the Boeing stopped twice to let other aircraft past. There was time to inspect the planes, twisted and abandoned, parked at the runway's margin, and the edges of previous runways, now cracking and overgrown and disappearing into the red earth.

In the terminal building there was time to observe the fruits of Angolans' shopping trips to Johannesburg – a bubble-wrapped coffee table, a child's tricycle – spewed forth on the luggage belt, and to take note of Angolan rich teen fashion: a boy with his hair bleached platinum blond, wearing a white shirt; another, his hair thick and black, dressed all in black, with the thinnest chinstrap beard bleached platinum blond. Outside, in the glaring light, I made out the sign held by Anabela Brandão, whose family had been playing host to journalists for nearly a decade.

Anabela seized one of my bags and marched towards the car, yelling as she went at the urchins who clustered around us trying to offer their services as porters. The route out of the airport took us around a traffic island decorated with fountains and monumental sculptures inspired by central African woodcarving. Beyond that, evidence of urban maintenance disappeared, the car churning through pools of water in the flooded road. The rainy season was over; the flooding was the result of broken water mains.

I was given a room in the Brandãos' coral pink house that led onto the front veranda and afforded a glimpse of the Atlantic. Inside, the house was cool and tiled, its oddest feature the absence of an inside kitchen. Instead, there was a tiny room, little more than a lean-to, across the back yard, which in colonial times would have been the preserve of the servants. Even now, cooking and the rest of the house-work were the responsibility of Anabela's three adopted daughters, Carmita, Cândida and Hilda, and the *empregada* (maid), Emélia.

The seasons were changing, the winter beginning, but Luanda was still uncomfortably hot for a new arrival. Yet you had only to stand still for a second and a breeze would creep from the sea and make the temperature bearable again.

❖

A few days later, driving to a children's home on the outskirts of the city to speak to Isaura and the other survivors of the Caxito raid, I was able to observe up close the dusty expanse of urban settlement that I had seen from the air. From the ground the houses in the peri-urban neighbourhoods that make up most of Luanda still appeared to be shoved together, piled on top of one another, asymmetrical and randomly placed. Yet they were not shanties: their construction out of cement blocks made them into houses. Mortar oozed from between the unplastered blocks; and the zinc roofs were heaped with stones to stop them from blowing away. Water lay around in festering lakes among the houses. Those drainage ditches that existed were heaped full of garbage.

Angolans have two names for such areas. The first of these is *musseque*, which refers specifically to the jumble of home-made houses on the sand. The other word is *bairro*, which in Portugal refers to a neighbourhood, but in Angola has taken on the connotation of a poor neighbourhood. The message: the well-off live singly, the masters of their domain; the poor have to be content with neighbourhood, with community.

At the opposite extreme from the *bairros* was the Cidade Alta, the Upper City, the largest part of which was taken up by the Presidential Palace, a mini-Versailles in rose-coloured plaster. It was used for ceremonial purposes only, since President José Eduardo dos Santos preferred to spend most of his time at the seaside compound of Futungo de Belas. The palace and its surrounds were maintained, however, as a reminder that there was still a state, and it was still in charge.

At night, the presidential palace glowed above the rest of the city, its floodlights accounting for a substantial percentage of Luanda's total electricity consumption. Not that the palace was competing with ordinary consumers – it had its own generators, which meant that it still glowed even when a power cut had turned Luanda into a sea of darkness.

Between the Cidade Alta and the bay was the Cidade Baixa, the Lower City where colonial Luanda had begun. Its oldest buildings dated back to the seventeenth century, as did the narrow streets.

Some buildings housed dusty shops on the ground floor, with dark staircases that led to flats above; others were roofless, blue sky visible as you looked from the street through their upper windows. Homeless children lived in the abandoned buildings, and bathed in the potholes where clear water bubbled up through the sandy earth from broken water pipes. The one modern building, a 14-storey tower, was distinguished at pavement level by a rare gesture of political dissidence: employees of the state shipping company, Angonave, had held a round-the-clock vigil for more than six months, demanding back-pay that they were owed when the company went bankrupt. They had painted slogans on brown cardboard, and tied them to the pillars. One placard compared the Angolan government to Hitler, Idi Amin, and the Portuguese dictator António Salazar, who in the 1960s had refused the independence of the colonies.

Scattered around the Baixa, signboards with the names of Portuguese contractors marked out the building sites. Even while the war continued inland and out of sight, there was enough confidence in the capital city to allow reconstruction to begin and to become a useful source of revenue for the old coloniser's building firms.

One of these new buildings, as it took shape from concrete blocks, was starting to acquire the ornate fluted window frames of the older buildings. In the eighteenth century, the site had been the home of Dona Ana Joaquina Santos: a mixed-race woman, and one of Angola's most famous slave traders. Dona Ana had lived on the top floor, slaves were held on the ground floor, and the lady's offices were in the middle. At the beginning of the present century, a governmental mix-up caused the building – one of Luanda's most distinctive historical monuments – to be demolished. An air-conditioned concrete replica was commissioned apologetically. The slaver's house was destined for use as a court of law.

Alta, Baixa, in between, or wherever you went in Luanda, the mausoleum was hard to avoid. This concrete space-rocket, built as a monument to the late President Agostinho Neto on the low-lying ground behind the Cidade Alta, was tall enough to protrude above the hilltop into almost any city vista even though its base was on low-lying ground. Neto had died in 1979. Twenty-two later, the mausoleum was still not complete, and two cranes were as much part of the skyline as the grey spike itself.

Up close, it was still less impressive. Shacks nudged its perimeter, pigs and goats browsing in the rubbish that was piled against the boundary fence. This detour to inspect the mausoleum was the first stop on a night-time guided tour of the area given to me by Rafael Marques: someone I had heard of before I ever arrived in Angola. Two years earlier, Marques had been imprisoned for writing an article about President José Eduardo dos Santos entitled 'The lipstick of dictatorship'. It was his case, more than any other, that drew international attention to the practices of a regime that had been feted by the international left in the 1970s and 1980s, and then embraced by oil-thirsty western governments in the 1990s. His imprisonment had aroused enough indignation abroad to persuade the Angolan authorities to suspend his sentence.

Rafael lived not far from the mausoleum in Bairro Azul, a middle-class neighbourhood at the back of the Cidade Alta. Its name, literally 'Blue Neighbourhood', reflected the original Portuguese meaning of *bairro*, before the term took on the Angolan connotation of a slum. We set off in the Landcruiser that belonged to the Open Society Initiative for which Rafael worked, bumping along the street, which even in this salubrious quarter had not been repaired for decades. No matter. Luxury four-wheel-drive vehicles, designed for rough rural conditions, had in Angola become standard issue for many non-governmental organisations, even those whose work was confined to the cities. Such vehicles were also available in a version with tinted windows and magnesium alloy hubcaps, which had become the car of choice for wealthy Angolans.

After circling the mausoleum's shacks and livestock we continued south, away from the city centre. A traffic roundabout marked the end of Bairro Azul where a bridge was being built to carry the main flow of traffic over the intersection. There was a simple reason for its construction: this was the quickest route between the official presidential palace on the hill and the unofficial one at Futungo de Belas.

Beyond the roundabout the streets became narrower, and if the tarmac in Bairro Azul was broken, here the road seemed never to have been tarred. The road surface, moreover, was a clear 30 centimetres above the level of people's front yards. The presidential hill was slowly burying the *bairro*: a few decades of rain had washed the silt downhill and stacked it up on top of what had once been a tarred road. Now when it rained, the water ran straight off the road and into people's houses. Rafael was building a new house for his mother, and had ordered the builders to put the house on a raised foundation so it would form a dry island during the rains. Meanwhile, the roadworks at the junction meant that the neighbourhood had had neither water nor electricity for several months.

Returning to the hill, we drove up past an elegantly restored colonial building: it had been a convent, but the nuns had seen the economic sense in letting it out to Sonangol, the state oil company, while they moved into cheaper accommodation out of town. At the summit, a floodlit water tower was painted in pink and white to match the presidential palace. It was meant for the exclusive use of the palace and its surrounding buildings, so that the dignitaries would never have to suffer water cuts.

Bairro Azul itself had attracted a small share of presidential largesse – a park with neat lawns, swings and a slide for children. A brass plaque revealed this to be the work of the Eduardo dos Santos Foundation (FESA), the president's private charity. With its access to foreign expertise and few restraints on its budget, FESA got things done in a country where government services barely functioned.

That Dos Santos presided over a moribund administration was of lesser consequence when the president's name was riveted onto the few public projects that did get completed. If there were ever any discontent around his regime's incompetence, all he had to do was to come to the rescue by sacking the minister involved. On one occasion in the 1990s, his response to four-digit inflation had been to arrive at a Luanda supermarket, accompanied by television cameras, express shock at the food prices and, the next day, dismiss the finance minister.

In Bairro Azul, the personal touch went further. At one end of the park was a kindergarten, its walls decorated with cartoon-style children of various colours, the girls with regulation pigtails and the teacher with regulation granny-glasses and hair in a bun. The name of the kindergarten was 'Zédu', the affectionate nickname for José Eduardo.

Much later, I read *Fast Food Nation*, Eric Schlosser's analysis of America's corporate hamburger and chicken industry. The economy that Schlosser describes seems a long way from Angola's mixture of subsistence agriculture, petro-capitalism and donor aid. Yet his book includes a photograph of a primary school class rapt before an actor dressed as Ronald McDonald, the burger chain's clown mascot. With the Zédu kindergarten Dos Santos's advisors had given the presidency a dose of McDonalds-style marketing.

FESA was also closely linked to ADPP, the Danish charity that ran the school in Caxito. The logic of the war was such that some Luandans reckoned UNITA would have seen this fact alone as sufficient justification for its kidnap raid on the town.

Nobody expected the Caxito children to be found alive. Yet one Friday lunchtime, almost three weeks after the kidnapping, Rádio Ecclésia reported a statement from UNITA that the children had been handed over to the church in the town of Negage in Uige province in the north. I managed to get through on the phone to the archdiocesan office in Uige, listening to my own bad Portuguese echoing back down the line. Yes, a priest told me, 60 children had been released and, while their identities still had to be confirmed, they were believed to be the same children who had disappeared from Caxito.

According to UNITA's statement the capture of the children had been an error, contrary to the rules governing the conduct of UNITA soldiers. Given that the kidnap and conscription of minors had long been a commonplace of UNITA military strategy, such an assertion seemed cynical even by the normal standards of wartime propaganda. But it was no less plausible than the official version that emerged only several hours later. When Rádio Ecclésia interviewed an officer from the Angolan Armed Forces (FAA), he insisted that the children had been liberated by the FAA in the course of a battle against UNITA.

In addition to the official palace, and the estate out at Futungo (and, it was said, substantial property interests in Portugal and Brazil), President dos Santos had at least one other property in Luanda. It was in the cliff-top ambassadorial district of Miramar, overlooking the slum of Boavista where, two months after my arrival in Luanda, the army and police were to evict the residents in the name of property development.

Before then, however, there occurred an event of cosmic importance – large enough at any rate to get Dos Santos to leave Luanda. He rarely appeared in public, and the only time he ever left the capital was when he left Angola, whether on a state visit or on a holiday to one of those other Portuguese-speaking lands across the sea. Getting him to the Angolan provinces required the total solar eclipse of 21 June 2001.

The path of the total eclipse was to stretch across southern Africa from west to east, starting over the Atlantic and reaching the Angolan coast at Sumbe, the capital of Kwanza Sul province, 300 kilometres south of Luanda. More remarkably, Angola was to experience a second total eclipse only 18 months later, in December 2002.

The approaching event provided a ripe opportunity for the government to be seen to be doing something. Billboards appeared on a few prominent corners in Luanda: 'The eclipse is marvellous, your eyes are precious.' The local media spoke of six million pairs of protective glasses being imported, of which two million were to be given away for free to needy communities. I visited a settlement of Congolese refugees on the outskirts of the city on a day when the deputy minister of social services, Maria de Luz, paid a visit to dispense such glasses. There weren't enough to go around. The minister was nearly trampled by the crowd, even though the refugees were not intending to watch the eclipse anyway.

One old matron, in fact, sounded as though the event had been organised especially to vex her. 'I'm going to stay inside and close the door,' she fumed.

Outside the capital, it was proving even more difficult to get the message across. 'Savimbi will probably appear out of the bush and tell everyone he commands the sun,' was the assessment of Mike McDonagh, an Irish aid agency director who had been familiar with the ways of the UNITA leader since the siege of Kuito eight years earlier. Despite the irony, the remark captured the aura of mythical awe with which Jonas Savimbi was regarded by allies and by enemies, in Angola and abroad.

Even the loyal *Jornal de Angola* was unable to be completely optimistic about the country's readiness for viewing an eclipse in time of war, revealing, for example, that in the weeks before the eclipse the information campaign in Cunene province was delayed because the regional airport was out of commission. From the town of Cubal in Benguela province the authorities expressed concern that the eclipse campaign material had not arrived – hardly surprising, since Cubal had been cut off from the outside world while the FAA engaged in a campaign against UNITA. The *Jornal* quoted a government official who had issued a statement underlining the importance of 'tolerance, harmony and national reconciliation' when it came to observing natural phenomena.

The press were more enthusiastic, meanwhile, about the arrest of a certain unnamed foreign national, accused of importing 5 350 illegal pairs of sunglasses. Forensic tests had revealed that the glasses were not up to the Angolan government's standards; infrared rays had been shown to penetrate the lenses, which meant the glasses were a threat to anyone who might wear them to look at the eclipse.

In light of the warning United Nations staff had been given not to drive to Sumbe, my main concern was how to get there at all. With flying the only option, I set off for the airport in the early hours of the morning of 21 June with Colin McClelland, the Reuters correspondent – not the important international terminal, its entrance marked by the roundabout with fountains and monumental statues, but the domestic terminal, which was somewhere down a road that branched off the roundabout to the left. Leading off that road there were a number of unmarked, unlit lanes, any one of which might just have been the access road. We proceeded by trial and error – the least likely looking one ended up being the right road: .a roadscape with particularly impressive lakes and mountains. Inside the airport, only one third of the fluorescent light tubes worked, just enough to attract abundant winged insects into the gloom. Domestic air travel was not a priority for the Luanda authorities.

For Sumbe, on the other hand, the eclipse was a rare moment of fame, and the airport had been painted pink for the occasion. It was draped with banners with the slogan 'Welcome to the capital of the sun', depicting waterfalls, the Luanda skyline, and pretty girls holding baskets of fruit of a lustre seen only on the shelves of the importers' supermarkets. The immigration officials had been kitted out with tailored black trench coats. One of them had the task of copying every passenger's passport details into an exercise book.

Outside, the reception for the president was waiting in neat rows. I asked one white-shirted primary school boy what he could tell me about the eclipse. He had it pat: 'The eclipse is a natural phenomenon in which the moon passes in front of the sun ...' The local members of the Angolan Women's Organisation – the women's league of the MPLA – were there in their yellow satin headscarves and red T-shirts. Party officials were leading the singing and chanting as they handed out sunglasses.

Dos Santos, amigo
O povo está contigo
(Dos Santos, friend, the people are with you.)
Snipers stood guard on the airport roof.

When it came to commanding the sun, the party machinery ensured that Dos Santos was doing it far more effectively than Savimbi could ever hope to.

Even then we didn't get to see the president; the bus taking passengers to the viewing site by the sea was leaving before Dos Santos's plane landed. We headed into town, past a banner strung across the street of a drab-looking *bairro: Welcome to the capital of the sun*. Cresting the hill that separates the town from the seashore, we reached the viewing site on top of a headland. It had recently been colonised by a new tourist complex: a cluster of prefabricated cabins, and a pavilion where Portuguese Sagres beer and Johnny Walker Red Label scotch were being handed out to anyone who had arrived on the plane.

Down below on the beachfront, two concrete hotels, their pastel paint barely dry, faced the esplanade, which had been strung around with fairy lights and lined with palm-thatched restaurants: a textbook riviera surrounded by a war zone. The UN's warnings about not driving to Sumbe had been ignored by Luanda's car-owning classes. Parked on the beach were shiny four-by-fours laden with picnic baskets and crates of imported beer. The BBC *Focus on Africa* programme had asked for an interview with an Angolan in English on the subject of the eclipse, and I reckoned that if I were to find an English-speaking Angolan in Sumbe, it was more likely to be among these *mestiço* day-trippers than among the locals. Golden-haired, blue-eyed Siza volunteered.

Over the course of an hour, the light faded bit by bit. Then it was as though someone had flicked a switch. Cheers broke out as the sky turned dark blue with a black disc surrounded by silver flames where the sun had been. The four minutes of totality experienced in Sumbe made it an unusually long event – just as well, since I spent much of the time trying to get the satellite phone to work so as to capture some spontaneous wonderment from the onlookers.

I linked up Siza with *Focus on Africa* within minutes of the daylight starting to drift back. Afterwards she kissed me shyly on both cheeks and her father offered me a cold Heineken from his stocks. I asked him about the road trip from Luanda. 'The road was safe,' he said. It seemed the FAA, even if it could not stop UNITA from kidnapping children from schools, could at least make a public highway safe for picnickers.

An elderly, bearded white man approached and wanted to talk. He was from the Netherlands, and revealed that he had been the one arrested on charges of illegal sunglass importation. His glasses complied with European Union regulations, he said, but this had apparently not been good enough for Angolan customs. His primary mission in Angola, however, was not to sell sunglasses, but to spread the good news of the eclipse; or, rather, of the rare phenomenon of two eclipses crossing the same territory within a period of only 18 months.

'I have written to President dos Santos suggesting that the 18 full moons between the two eclipses should be a time to reflect on national reconciliation and draft a new constitution,' he explained.

And Dos Santos's reaction? The Dutchman said he had received a 'diplomatic' reply.

On the way back to the airport, the bus broke down next to a bit of graffiti that said *Savimbi quer paz* (Savimbi wants peace). People were passing around cold beer, and Johnny Walker on the rocks – somehow, they still had ice by that stage of the day. We arrived at the airport to find the plane had a flat tyre.

The delay meant that we finally got to see Dos Santos. We were all herded inside the airport building before the presidential motorcade – which had been driven down from Luanda for the occasion – arrived from the direction of the town and parked on the runway side of the terminal building. As we watched through the plate glass windows, a tall figure, shoulders slightly hunched, got out of the car. Without breaking stride, he glanced over towards the people watching from inside, and offered a nervous wave. The half-smile on the president's face seemed almost embarrassed. Then he took the red-carpeted path to the aircraft steps, boarded, and the plane taxied for take-off without a moment's delay.

'*Quem quer peixe?*' Who wants fish?

Luanda's women fish-vendors had a way of making their voices into klaxons, carrying on their heads baskets or bowls from which dead fish-eyes stared skywards. They started at dawn from the Ilha, the island – that long spit of land that separates Luanda Bay from the Atlantic. The Ilha is joined to the mainland by a causeway at its southern end linking it to the Cidade Baixa. To the right, houses and shacks seemed to tumble into the water of the harbour; to the left lay the dirty beaches where the fishermen launched their boats.

The northernmost section of the Ilha had been cordoned off in the old days and access permitted only to senior MPLA members and Cuban *cooperantes*. In the new, capitalist Angola, market forces were proving an equally effective way of maintaining the class divisions. Along the western, ocean-facing side of the Ilha, the beach had been divided up among a series of expensive restaurants and bars with sunset views, one of them owned by Isabela dos Santos, the president's daughter. Five-dollar cocktails and ten-dollar hamburgers kept the proletariat at a distance. The working-class beaches faced east, onto the polluted waters of the harbour. Every Sunday, muscular youths would practise their backward somersaults on these beaches, running in reverse and then launching themselves into the surf.

It was the Ilha that dominated the view from the mainland, whether you were up in the cliff-top ambassadorial suburb of Miramar, or standing at sea-level on the Marginal – the esplanade where expatriate joggers maintained a steady pace to leave muggers behind – or living in the less salubrious neighbourhood of Boavista that straggled down the hill below Miramar. On a warm winter's afternoon, the sun would silhouette the island's palm trees, drawing a line between the flat harbour and the Atlantic breakers; beyond that, the next stop was Brazil. With your back to the land, you could forget you were in a country whose recent history was defined by one of the nastiest civil wars of the late twentieth century. Yet those same sea views were to spark the biggest *confusão* that Luanda had seen in years.

Several of the World Food Programme's expatriate employees lived in Miramar, and the first rumblings of the events that were to overtake Boavista came in a WFP security memo forwarded by a staff member, warning that the government was about to start moving people from Boavista to a site somewhere out of town. The residents were not happy about this, the memo added, cautioning that 'those who have firearms are expected to use them'. The evictions were due to begin on Sunday 1 July.

That Sunday I tramped across the lower city, past the port, past the lemon-coloured colonial building that was the barely functioning railway station to where the tumbledown *musseque* houses marked the lower end of Boavista. A crowd prevented me from getting any further. From the shouting I could detect one refrain emerging from the shouting: *Casa para casa – não casa para tenda* – a house for a house, not a house for a tent. Were they to be evicted? In asking I mistakenly used the verb *deslocar* (displace) instead of *desalojar* (evict). The reaction was indignant: 'We are not *deslocados*.' The residents of Boavista wanted to make it clear that they, self-sufficient urban residents, were not part of the masses of displaced people whom the war had forced off their farms in the countryside.

Some government officials beckoned me away, to their car, and asked what I wanted. I wanted to know what the government was up to. For a response it appeared I had to speak to the provincial vice-governor himself, and I was driven to an office up on Miramar where I met Simão Paulo, not in his own office but in a lesser municipal building with a creaky wooden staircase and nothing more than a desk and two chairs in each room. This was not the presidential palace; this was how government really functioned, when it functioned, in Angola.

'During the last rainy season the area became unsafe,' Paulo explained. 'So we decided to move the population to a more secure location.'

Boavista was on a steep and sandy hill, the kind of place where a heavy shower of rain might be able to undermine the foundations of a house. But the 'secure location' that the vice-governor was talking about was 40 kilometres away, beyond the satellite town of Viana. The 10 000 families of Boavista were to be given a pile of building materials and a tent to live in while they constructed homes on the new site. The anger of the people of Boavista was hardly surprising.

Paulo disagreed, however. 'These people do not want to participate,' he said with some irritation. 'They will be given building materials.'

The next day, Sunday, the first shots were fired at Boavista. A stout teenager called Cândida recalled later how she had been washing the dishes in her family's backyard when a bullet had embedded itself in her thigh. The state media reported that it was Boavista residents themselves who had fired the shots. Thirteen people had been arrested and charged with 'agitation'. Whoever was really behind the shooting, there was no doubt that there were plenty of firearms concealed under beds and on top of wardrobes in Boavista. The government knew this very well. It was the government that had handed out weapons to MPLA supporters during the elections in 1992.

Some of the houses at Boavista were indeed as precarious as Simão Paulo had portrayed them. The steepest part of the Boavista cliff was constituted of garbage as much of sand, a rubbish tip that had become fossilised. The shacks built on top seemed no less flimsy than the plastic bags that sprouted from the cliff edge. But further back from the cliff the ground was solid and the houses equally sturdy, built of cement blocks, not shanties. Many of them were painted in the pastel colours that accompany the Portuguese language wherever it is planted around the globe; some were decorated with patterns of shells that the builders had pressed into the cement while it was wet. Now someone had slapped crosses of black paint on top of the pastel colours and the shells.

Mrs Verdadeira had spent US $ 9 000 on her house, and it still was not finished. A gilt plastic clock and a calendar with photographs of flowers hung on the unpainted walls. Her large voice grated along the narrow cement corridor as she showed off her home: 'A lounge, three bedrooms, a bathroom, a kitchen. If they are to move us, let it be on the basis of a house for a house, not a house for a tent.'

It was Saturday again, a week after my first visit to Boavista. David Mendes, the lawyer who was defending the 13 men who had been arrested, took me along to introduce me to some of the people whose homes were under threat. Mrs Verdadeira had the documents proving that she had paid taxes on her land.

A rundown but much loved settlement on a hill overlooking a harbour; a government that was determined to pull down the houses and move people to dusty flatlands far from the city. This summary of the situation at Boavista could, 35 years earlier, have been applied to Cape Town's District Six, a neighbourhood whose destruction has become one of the icons of the injustice of apartheid. Here in Angola was a government that had prided itself on its opposition to apartheid and its concern for human progress ('most important is to solve the problems of the people' in the words of a slogan from the seventies) acting in the manner of its old adversary in the south.

On Sunday, one week after the first shootings and arrests, the police arrived in force. Horsemen were lined up on the road that ran along the top of the cliff; more policemen stood around, some in riot helmets, all with guns. In front of them was a drop of about ten metres to the first flat terrace where the *bairro* began. Men with sledgehammers were already destroying people's homes, whack by whack. In the distance, Mrs Verdadeira's bright orange shirt stood out. She stood still among the throngs of people who were starting to move mattresses, chairs, tables, electric fans, and load them onto the yellow trucks that were waiting. People were climbing onto the trucks on top of their furniture.

Rafael Marques, whose office was nearby, was there too and together we started down the path towards the houses. Halfway, we were confronted by a hulk of a man who pushed us around, called Rafael a mercenary, and said a lot else that was beyond the scope of my Portuguese. We left. I never got another chance to talk to Mrs Verdadeira.

We went back later in the week, accompanied by José Rasgadinho, the chairman of the residents' committee. The upper part of Boavista was now a calm ocean of rubble. We spoke to the people whose houses still bore black crosses, next in line for demolition. Among them was an officer from the Angolan Armed Forces who had had to keep his children home from school, so distressed were they at the thought of losing their home. Another man said he had seen an elderly neighbour die from the stress of seeing her home pulled down. Youths with nothing else to do picked up chunks of cement and pelted them at a cat that darted across the debris.

'If this had happened in any other country in southern Africa, they would be throwing things at the police,' I said.

Rafael smiled. 'That's the strange thing about Angola.'

Given what happened at Boavista, the lack of public reaction indeed seemed extraordinary. When a church service and candlelit vigil in the ruins of Boavista were advertised for the following Sunday, the event was banned. Protest was something that the authorities did not expect, and which people barely felt they had a right to. Most of them, after their initial anger, got onto the yellow trucks with their possessions and made the journey to Zango.

The next day I went with Rafael and Rasgadinho to take a look at the site that the government had set aside for the residents of Boavista. It took the best part of two hours to get there, driving through Bairro Popular, a neighbourhood distinguished by its buried car parts: springs and engine blocks emerging from the earth. For a few kilometres we drove parallel to Luanda's only working railway line, people riding goods wagons on rails that looked as though they were lying out with the garbage rather than fixed to the ground. At Viana town we turned off onto a dirt road, past some scraggy fields of cassava, past the shantytowns that accommodated the real *deslocados*: the victims of the war. Here people from Kwanza Sul, there people from Malange, over there people from Moxico – an Angolan geography in miniature, marked out in corrugated iron and flapping plastic.

The site reserved for the people from Boavista suggested that they too were suddenly *deslocados*, however much they may have resisted the term less than a fortnight before. Khaki tents sagged into the red dust. Outside some of the tents was a table the size of a footstool where someone was trying to sell a handful of onions or a few tins of tomato paste. A portable generator powered a single street lamp at the end of each row. Arranged around the perimeter – a clear hundred metres from the most centrally placed tents – were toilet blocks. Further away, a single half-constructed showhouse stood next to a site where people dug trenches for new foundations.

Within moments, two policemen had appeared. They shook hands politely and wished us good morning, but the size of their automatic weapons left no doubt as to the wisdom of making ourselves scarce. We drove over to look at the building site of the single half-finished house that had been shown on television as the Boavista of the future. Again we were stopped. A junior government official explained to us, almost apologetically: 'In other countries there is press freedom, but not in Angola.' The same view was expressed more subtly the next morning by the MPLA information secretary, Norberto dos Santos, when he held a rare briefing for journalists in Luanda. When I told him about our two encounters with the police in the past week, he assured me that the press in Angola was free. It was just that we had to get permission from the authorities when covering certain stories.

A group of parliamentarians seemed to provide enough such authority, so that afternoon I joined a delegation of MPs who were visiting the Zango camp. As I wandered among the tents and talked to people, the government's strategy became clearer. There were no labourers on hand to build the promised new houses. The former residents of Boavista, who had paid thousands of dollars for houses that were then knocked down, were now being forced to work, unpaid, to build new ones.

'We have become workers for the government,' said a man called Baptista. 'If people resist they take our names and we don't have the right to a house. If we don't work we don't have the right to a house.'

Catarina, a tiny woman, seemed caught up in a rage that was bigger than she was. 'In Boavista, I used to sell things in the market to make a living. Survival here depends on the government,' she said. 'It's slavery – they are enslaving the people.'

She had had to abandon her market stall, her only source of income, since she could not afford the bus fare to town and back.

Now she was dependent on government handouts – '25 kilos of maize, 25 kilos of sugar, 25 kilos of rice' – handouts that she said were given only to those who worked on the building site. Daily roll calls kept tabs on who was present to work, and who had slipped off to seek employment in town.

While we were talking, two armed policemen walked over to Rafael, escorted him to a police truck, and drove him away. David Mendes and the others with him were nowhere to be seen. A government official in a sagging blouse and lopsided hair scolded me about people coming from the outside and disrupting things.

'We were invited by the people who lived here,' I pointed out.

'Who crucified Christ?' she asked.

'Pontius Pilate?' I ventured.

'It was the people who crucified Christ,' she corrected me. 'The people are always demanding things. If you had children you would know that children are always demanding things. They do not care how their father is earning his money.'

The 'people's movement' that supposedly constituted Angola's ruling party seemed a long way away. Once again, the scene was uncomfortably reminiscent of apartheid South Africa. Reminiscent too of Gerald Bender's book *Angola under the Portuguese*, in which he describes how the colonial rulers herded black Angolans into resettlement villages as a measure against insurgency during the independence war. The difference here was that the bullying bureaucrat was *mestiça*; in South Africa, or in colonial Angola, she would have been white and almost certainly male.

Mendes eventually came back from the other side of the camp. I took out my mobile phone to call *Focus on Africa*, which was about to go on air, and tell them that Rafael Marques was in custody once again. A policeman told me to put the phone away, but Mendes managed to call Rádio Ecclésia. It was getting dark and cold. Mendes switched on his car radio and we huddled in the dusk around the dim light of the car listening to the muttered Hail Marys in Portuguese in the run-up to the news bulletin.

Rafael appeared about an hour later. Mendes had persuaded one of the bureaucrats to call the police and ask for his release.

Later, our troubles with the authorities at Boavista and at Zango reached the attention of press freedom activists in Europe and the United States. They also reached the ears of Joffre Justino, a UNITA sympathiser in Lisbon who would occasionally send mass e-mails detailing unlikely rebel victories against government forces. This time, however, his communication had a personal touch.

Meu Caro,

Solidário com o direito à informação lamento o que lhe sucedeu, a si e ao Rafael.

Um abraço,

Joffre Justino

(My dear, Believing in the right to information, I am sorry about what happened to you, and to Rafael too. An embrace. Joffre Justino)

From Angolan Public Television, the only station available to those who lacked satellite dishes, came a different view of the Boavista removals. The news report showed a woman delighted with her tent, telling how here in the camp she was free from the rats that had bothered her in Boavista. And a book and a website suggested that there were at least tentative future plans for the site.

The book, with colour photographs on glossy paper, had been published several months earlier by the state oil company, Sonangol. It told of plans by Sonangol's subsidiary oil services company, Sonils, to develop the area around Luanda harbour. As well as a base for Sonils, the development would include 'the construction of a shopping centre, a residential area with entertainment clubs, restaurant, bar, leisure areas, supermarket, swimming pool, laundry and cable television'. An editorial described the project as a 'challenge that requires a joint solution with the provincial government of Luanda to construct an economic residential area to relocate the people who inhabit the area surrounding the base. We will succeed.'

The website, on the other hand, purported to have been put up by a venture called 'Consulted'. It advertised a complex of 583 flats with 'the best views in Luanda in the heart of the city'. 'Consulted' could be consulted care of CNC, the Angolan state cargo shipping company. Financial management was being carried out by Dar Al-Handasah Consultants, a company that happened to be headed by Ramzi Klink who also chaired the finance committee of the Dos Santos Foundation.

Caxito and Boavista. These two events, respectively the actions of a brutal rebel movement and a brutal government, between them encompassed the stubborn hopelessness of wartime Angola. One expects repressive governments to give rise to dissidence and, given the necessary material support, dissidence can solidify into armed rebellion. This is not what happened in Angola. The country was long overdue for a change of government, but UNITA was not the alternative that Angola needed.

In any case, UNITA had not come into being because people were fed up with the MPLA. UNITA was the enemy extraordinaire of the Angolan state only by virtue of the fact that UNITA and the MPLA had been rival liberation movements 25 years earlier. In mirror fashion, the MPLA's claim to legitimacy in government derived from the same period. The MPLA had subsequently been elected as the majority party in parliament in 1992. It was the country's only multi-party poll, but one in which the MPLA had held all the advantages of an incumbent, including a monopoly over the state media. Since 1992, war had provided a convenient excuse for not having any elections at all.

So the question of Angola's future was still defined, still polarised, by two rival movements dating from the period before independence. Back then, the history books will have us believe, the MPLA and UNITA represented, respectively, the interests of the Portuguese-speaking people of the coast and the Umbundu-speaking people of the Central Highlands. These days, it was difficult to recognise whose interests, if any, either side was defending.

Neither UNITA nor the FAA was fighting for anybody's freedom. The real conflicts of interest in Angola – between poor city-dwellers and government autocrats or, as I would later discover, between unarmed peasants and soldiers from either or both armies

– did not even appear on the political map. Oblivious, the war continued under its own momentum.

After a civilian car ran over an anti-tank mine in the Central Highlands, a priest interviewed on the radio described it as *'um crescendo de confusão'.*

2

It's hard to believe we're in the same country

Kuito airport was already in sight before the plane started to drop down from its cruising altitude of 30 000 feet. Then it flipped over onto its side and we descended in a gut-wrenching spiral. This was a standard security procedure for United Nations planes in most of Angola. Airspace below 30 000 feet was reckoned to be at risk from surface-to-air missiles. Pilots were allowed to descend below this altitude only after they had entered the safe zone that extended for a radius of 20 kilometres around each town.

At that phase of the Angolan civil war, there was no chance of doing what journalists are supposed to do and visit the front line. The certainty of such a concept had disappeared two years earlier, when the Angolan Armed Forces (FAA) had recaptured Andulo and Bailundo, Jonas Savimbi's last bastions in the Planalto Central – the Central Highlands, the region UNITA considered its own. With the fall of those towns, the nature of the war had changed from a struggle for the control of territory to a fast-moving and unpredictable guerrilla conflict in which the rebels appeared to have the strategic advantage. UNITA and the FAA were chasing each other round in small circles all over the Planalto; an attempt to find the front line would have induced a rapid attack of dizziness.

Every day, hundreds of people would arrive from the country-side, seeking food and shelter in the larger Planalto towns: Kuito and Camacupa and Huambo. In the ten years since the war resumed, four million people had already lost their homes. In the language of the aid agencies they had become *deslocados*, the dislocated, the displaced. Only later, after several more trips to Kuito and points east, would I discover that these people were not simply those who had escaped the crossfire; their very existence was the key to the military strategies not only of UNITA, but of the government too.

The closest one could get to the war was to speak to its survivors – or its victims, depending on which way one looked at it. This was why I found myself in the fumey dawn, on a road full of thundering oil trucks and minibuses, headed for the military section of Luanda's airport and a seat on one of the World Food Programme's 12-seater passenger planes that flew between Luanda and the provincial towns.

Inside the air force compound was a warehouse that served as a passenger waiting room, not only for the WFP's guests but also for people who had begged or bribed their way onto military Antonov transport planes. In Angola, state property was at the disposal of whichever official might be in charge of it and, since most of the money in state coffers went to the military, it was army officers who commanded the most useful assets, particularly transport. Military planes formed the backbone of Angola's internal commerce. Officers would sell plane rides to traders, who staggered on board with whatever they could carry.

The quantity of our luggage made a clear distinction between the Antonov and the WFP passengers. Those who were flying with the army had boxes and bags equal to their own body weight, all done up with kilometres of parcel tape. The rest of us had our allotted 12 kilograms of luggage, weighed on an old fashioned balance by Luisa, a stern-faced young Angolan with a khaki cap and a walkie-talkie. My fellow passengers were aid workers and two nuns. The pilots were white South Africans who talked blithely about 'flying just above the missile envelope' as they cruised over an ocean of grass of a colour somewhere between gold and silver that was the Planalto in mid-winter.

Down to Kuito, the plane pirouetting on its right wingtip. Through the left portholes the sky; through the right the earth, Kuito and Kuito's runway, looking like a road in a Luanda *bairro*, or a large fossilised piece of Swiss cheese. That runway had become famous. Foreign aid donors had been complaining that the state of the runway meant that Kuito was barely getting half of the emergency food stocks it needed. As the runway spun like a propeller in our field of vision, I reached for my camera. It felt like a brick – a matter of G forces.

Eight years earlier, while Huambo, the biggest town on the Planalto, fell to UNITA after a 55-day siege, Kuito had remained in government hands. Although the townsfolk had come out in support of UNITA in the September 1992 elections, they resisted the rebels' attempts to take the city by force after Savimbi rejected the results of the elections and returned to war. Cut off from the agricultural land surrounding the town, bands of people would fight their way past UNITA lines at night, and roam the landmine-sown countryside to gather food. The stand-off between UNITA and the FAA in Kuito lasted for nine months, and for much of that time it was Kuito's main road that formed the front line. There were said to be 30 000 bodies buried in Kuito's parks and back gardens.

Driving into Kuito from the airport, evidence of that struggle was written along the road in the remains of houses built during a wave of Portuguese settlement in the middle of the twentieth century. At a time when the British and French were pulling out of Africa, the Portuguese had been heading for the colonies faster than ever before. In 1955, only 60 000 whites lived in Angola; by 1975, their numbers had grown to 335 000, a four-fold increase in 20 years. Some stayed in the flats and townhouses of Luanda. Others had ended up on the plateau, their homes put together out of cast concrete, as if with a child's construction kit, and painted Toyland colours to match. Now the big toys had been smashed.

Kuito's central square, dating from earlier in the twentieth century, had been designed to impress. On its western side was a stately crescent of three government buildings, built in baroque style and painted the same pink as the presidential palace in Luanda. The Angolan flag flew over the one building of the three that was still intact. The other two showed blue sky through their rafters and piles of rubble through their empty windows.

Across the square were the remains of the church. The steeple was just about standing, but the nave had been reduced to two walls forming a roofless L-shape empty of pews, where children now played soccer. Nearby, as if disturbed at their ablutions, a pair of bronze nudes stood coyly at an empty ornamental pond. Residents referred to the bronzes, which had managed somehow to escape the crossfire undamaged, as 'as estátuas sem vergonha' – the statues without shame.

With the car's ignition switched off, Kuito was as quiet as a desert. The only other vehicles in the town belonged to humanitarian organisations or to the army. The drone of an engine might rise and then vanish. The background of noise that would distinguish an urban settlement from a wasteland was absent here. In the street, two men, on their knees, were whitewashing alternate kerbstones to maintain the pattern of white, grey, white, grey. Later I would come to know this as a characteristically Angolan approach to solving problems: Look after the details, and the bigger picture can wait for another day.

Near the main square I peeked through a mortar hole in a building that had three and a half of its four walls intact. Inside, children were sitting in neat rows on milk-powder tins or home-made stools, rapt before a teacher. The schoolmaster wore a tie and a threadbare jacket, and was lecturing on the points of Portuguese grammar that he had chalked on the blackboard standing on an easel behind him. It was a schoolroom scene out of a storybook. The only detail missing was a roof.

Along the main street, the floors of a concrete office block, perhaps four or five storeys high, had collapsed at one end and concertinaed to the ground. The effect was that of a cross-section from a book on geomorphology showing how volcanic strata are tilted and warped by seismic upheaval, though here the strata were decorated with tiles. At the other end of the building, where the floors and ceilings were still roughly parallel, people were still living.

What was it like living in Kuito eight years after the siege and the war showing no signs of ending?

'*Mais ou menos.*'

Mais ou menos is literally 'more or less'. It is the Portuguese equivalent of 'so-so', a non-committal answer, and, like '*confusão*', is an example of the way Angolans take understatement all the way to the boundaries of calumny when they try to make an account of their daily realities. I heard it often in response to the phatic question 'How are you?' But never did I hear it uttered more poignantly than in Kuito.

The woman living in the concertinaed building did not try to exaggerate her situation because she had no need to. I was a journalist in search of pathos, and her answers to my questions were terse. 'The war destroyed our houses. There's not much money, not enough.'

'I hear life in Kuito is very expensive,' I ventured.

'Expensive, yes, very expensive, no,' she corrected me, adding as though by way of an afterthought: 'There isn't enough food. I have to make sacrifices to feed my children.'

For water, she had to walk more than a kilometre to the nearest stream: village life among the ruins of a town.

Gabriel was 17 years old, and carried an electronic keyboard more than half his own height. His father was an evangelical minister, which probably explained why Gabriel looked better fed than most of his neighbours. It certainly accounted for Gabriel having had enough of an education to be able to show off his English to me, and he obligingly turned out the kind of spiel that he thought journalists would be expecting:

'Life in Kuito is very difficult. It is hard because of war – the buildings are spoilt and destroyed – have no food, water, no electricity.'

His friend Israel also spoke some English, and gave me a literal translation of the Kuito mantra: 'Life in Kuito is more or less.'

❖

Like other foreign organisations in the town, WFP had located its offices in one of the former Portuguese settler homes. WFP's villa boasted a poinsettia tree in the yard, worn-out parquet floors, and an elegant staircase that swept in a curve from the reception area to the second-floor bedrooms, now offices. At the back was a feature that had not been envisaged by Kuito's colonial architects: a sandbagged subterranean bunker, in case things turned nasty again. A few days earlier, a shell had landed ten kilometres outside the town.

Two of the international agency's officials were visiting Kuito and invited me to tour the *deslocado* camps with them. We headed south along the front line main street, past the airport turn-off to where the suburban houses stopped, and the open country started. The road, sporadic tarmac between the potholes, cut a straight course across the undulating terrain.

Over the next hill, human habitation began again: huts that blanketed themselves over the hillside with the uniformity of grass. This was Kambendua, one of the post-1992 *deslocado* camps that were growing faster than ever before. In October of the previous year, 80 000 displaced people had been living in Kambendua and the other camps around Kuito. By May, the figure had doubled, and the state of the airport runway meant that there was not enough food to go around.

Grey-bearded Abel Sangueve was not charmed by the WFP officials' visit.

'When we arrived here they gave us food,' he complained, talking in Umbundo through the translation of a local WFP staff member. 'But it got less and less and we have had nothing for the last month.'

How had he come to be in a *deslocado* camp? The translator replied: 'They came because they were forced by UNITA. UNITA used to harass people, forcing them to join their army and asking people to contribute food for them. Whoever refused to do this was taken away to somewhere from where he will not return – probably they will be killed.'

There were no young or even middle-aged men in the camp. Between little boys, whose yellowing hair and swollen bellies betrayed malnutrition, and ageing patriarchs like Abel Sangueve there was a gaping hole in the male population. I asked the translator why.

'Most youths have gone for survival activity,' he explained.

This cryptic explanation did not match up with the more realistic version I had heard, namely that both warring armies practised forced conscription. If UNITA didn't get young men while they were in the bush, the FAA would round them up as soon as they arrived in town.

A few days later, after a plane flying for WFP came within range of an explosion in the sky, the UN cancelled cargo and passenger flights to all except a few destinations in Angola. For a while, I reported in my news despatches, no donor food got into Kuito at all.

We foreign journalists are too quick to believe what the aid agencies tell us. Even while UN security rules decreed that the only way into Kuito was by air, there was another set of rules as far as local commerce was concerned. Angolan truck drivers were still competing with the generals' Antonovs by taking the road from the coast to Huambo and thence to Kuito. Returning to Kuito a month after my first visit, sitting in a spare corner of the Oxfam office trying in vain to keep the sound of the generator out of my microphone, I spoke to Geraldo Jalo about his experiences moving freight between Huambo and Kuito.

'I have a fast truck, a Scania 112, and I used to be able to make the journey three times a week. But now, there is no security; I only go once a week. I can't be travelling constantly – because the ambushes take place constantly.'

Geraldo's recitation of casualties from UNITA attacks on the road between Kuito and Huambo included 23 deaths in the space of a few weeks. His catalogue of vehicle *marques*, locations and death tolls was relayed with precision: a Mazda burnt out between Boas Águas and Pedro Candungo; less than 24 hours later, a truck taking humanitarian aid to Kuito attacked and a child killed; four days later, an Efa lorry burnt and a mechanic killed; five days after that, a Soviet lorry attacked and two women killed.

His operating costs included not only fuel and tyres, but also 'mobilising the troops'. He meant, of course, slipping some cash to a local army officer who would then provide an escort. In Angola's flight from socialism, even the army was now for sale.

Divine intervention, however, came for free:

'I saw UNITA's men ten metres from the truck in front. I was saved by the grace of God. I was transporting literature for the Seventh Day Adventist Church for their conference. After three or four minutes the attackers suddenly disappeared.'

He continued: 'The pastor asked me "What is all this *confusão*?" I said to him: "That was an ambush."'

My real reason for a second trip to Kuito was not to interview truck drivers, but to make a road trip of my own. Humanitarian staff had begun setting up operations in Camacupa, a town about 80 kilometres north-east of Kuito, the direction from which most of the *deslocados* were arriving. For me there was the blunt fascination of a place that no journalist would have been to in years. But there was also the voyeuristic allure of getting closer to where the conflict appeared to be happening.

Flight schedules meant spending two days in Kuito before the road journey to Camacupa. I spent one at Kuito's new hotel, built in the shell of a six-storey building near the church and the administration buildings. The ground floor had once been an expansive café-bar, the counter fitted with display cabinets for cakes. Now there were about five bags of bread on the counter, and that was it.

I was led up a staircase and along a corridor worthy of a bombed-out building into a room where the paint was new, the net curtains were new, the bed was new, the bedcover was new, nylon and lurid pink. The bath had been filled up with water, thoughtfully so, since there was no running water. I had worked through the night before catching the dawn flight in Luanda, and I slept now until the late afternoon. Driven by thirst, I went downstairs to the big echoing breadshop to ask the owner if he could get me some drinking water. Half an hour later, he brought it up: a china coffee pot full of fresh spring water.

Bird watching was not an obvious hobby in a place like Kuito where anything made of flesh usually ended up in a pot, but Lewis McCaffrey, a laconic English water engineer with Oxfam, was a fan. Seeking wild fowl seemed a good enough excuse for a Planalto ramble and, with the assistance of three teenage freelance guides who attached themselves to us, we wandered through the *bairro* and up and down hills where — in a rare display of order and efficiency – the river had been canalised to power flour mills.

The boys took us to an elegantly curving dam with an impressive collection of non-functioning sluice gates. My fascination with industrial archaeology was quickly satisfied; Lewis the birdwatcher had to be content with a flock of sparrow-sized things that took off as our guides stomped towards them.

The three youths proved to be much better with military than with natural history.

'Here this path was full of bodies in 1993.'

'That hill was controlled by UNITA – this one was the government side.'

Next morning, the people in the Médecins sans Frontières (MSF) aid convoy to Camacupa were busy fixing flags onto the radio aerials of two Landcruisers and to a makeshift flagstaff attached to a ramshackle truck – an ambassadorial gesture, but in this case a protestation of neutrality: 'We're not UNITA, we're not the FAA, don't shoot us please.'

We started off on a road, sometimes gravel, sometimes axle-deep sand that took us through the bushveld, mostly burnt back on either side of the road in a swathe 20 to 500 metres wide. The dark tracks of the Benguela Railway – the line that had once crossed half a continent, connecting the ports of Benguela and Lobito with the mines of Zambia and the Congo — appeared and disappeared in the grass and earth. The last train went past here some time in the 1980s; the railway line had been a choice target for UNITA sabotage.

One village was surrounded by lush cultivation. '*Tem luz aquí*', (There's light here) someone said – it was the home village of a provincial official, hence the electricity. This and other villages were marked by FAA checkpoints, where a soldier would sit perched on an abandoned tank track or in a grass shelter. Bridges were no more than a couple of planks slung across the river. Invariably, the soldiers waved us through without a word.

We drove through Catabola, little more than a single street on the crest of a hill, colonial cottages in faded pastels with none of the pretentious bombast of Kuito's ruined suburbs. The windows were blank, and even the fact of people on the streets could not shake the impression of a place that was all but abandoned. 'This used to be Nova Sintra,' one of the Angolan staff remarked. Recalling colonial place names seemed to be a kind of 'I spy' game.

In Camacupa the trees, all mature specimens at least a few decades old, had had their branches pollarded for the winter, and their trunks were freshly whitewashed to a height of about a metre. Whether to repel insects or to warn drunken drivers at night, this practice was observed throughout the country with the same rigour as was applied to painting kerbstones in Kuito. Camacupa, however, showed little of the spectacular destruction of Kuito – instead of being bombarded, it had simply been left out to decay. A sign on a corner bar that looked as though no one had been served with a beer there in a long time proclaimed that this was the mid-point of Angola – a credible enough claim since most maps show Camacupa as close to the centre of the country as it is possible to get.

MSF had moved into the shell of a family house in Camacupa which was, bit by bit, acquiring doors, shutters, running water and generator-powered electricity. The staff would retire to the house for lunch each day, sitting in the back yard, under the papaya tree, on top of the underground bunker, where a rooster pecked around the pebbles, a scrap of metal tied to its claw to stop it from straying too far. Even this long after independence, in this far-flung former outpost of the Portuguese empire, Latin siesta rules persisted. Outside the house, a demented man hobbled around carrying a broad-bladed knife and the skeleton of an AK-47, chanting and groaning and making the kids laugh. A smug guy in an MPLA T-shirt rode by on a brand new bike and assured me life in Camacupa was good.

Visiting the *deslocado* camps was impossible without being accompanied by two half-drunk MPLA officials. Their presence meant that not even our translator was hearing an accurate account of people's stories. One man, asked why he had come to Camacupa, dared to state plainly: 'Because the government told us to.' The response was a chorus of shushing by his neighbours, led by our minders, who made it clear that you were not allowed to say things like that about the government.

It would take several more months before the army's strategy of emptying the countryside of farmers, whose fields were UNITA's larder, became clear.

At dawn the next day, the town's big empty pink school glowed in the early light. From another building, an abandoned shop perhaps, came the rhythmical shouts and grunts of group physical training: *capoeira*, the martial art that had been developed in Brazil by slaves brought from here, the centre of Angola.

Another day, and a visit to another *deslocado* camp where the people had arrived only weeks earlier and were still putting shelters together on the trampled, leafless earth. Again, we were unable to shake off the MPLA minder, this one in a bright yellow Camel T-shirt. The stories were the same as yesterday – UNITA forced us away from our villages. But these people all seemed to have gone first to Cuemba, the next town to the east. And they had no hesitation about telling us that they had left Cuemba because the local administration had told them to go. Some people – those who had arrived in the last day or two – were living around their fires with no roof between them and the highland winter days and nights. A nurse from MSF was screening children for malnutrition, assisted by yet another minder who, whenever a nursing mother was asked whether she had breast milk, took delight in giving a squeeze to check.

We drove back to Kuito the next day, the running commentary of the three Angolan aid workers in the vehicle lending a new perspective on the countryside. That bombed-out school? 1998. That wrecked tank? 1993. And, as we approached Kuito: 'UNITA was on this hill – the government was on that one.' They laughed and joked as they remembered.

I started asking them about the siege: 'How did you get by?'

'We stayed indoors during the day, only went out after the roadblocks had gone home for the night.'

'What did you eat?'

'Cats – rats.'

We were now on the outskirts of the city. 'UNITA got as far as this bridge in 1998' – 'No, not to this one' – 'Yes they did, and they made *grande confusão* in front of the police post.'

Some months later I was invited along on another brief trip to Kuito. The American ambassador, Christopher William Dell, was paying a call on Paulino dos Santos, the governor of Bié province, to try to find out why the airport runway had still not been fixed. It may seem strange for a matter of public works maintenance to be taken up at such a high diplomatic level, but the United States was matching its interest in Angolan oil with substantial food aid donations. The donor community was not allowed to contribute to the runway repairs since the airport was a military installation, and the potholes had been getting bigger for the last two years.

After a quick visit to the food distribution centre – where the MPLA party flag flew over the warehouse of donor maize – we assembled at the *palácio*, the gubernatorial residence, which proved to be in better condition than Kuito's shattered administration buildings. The members of the ambassador's delegation squeezed onto the fake leather sofas that were arranged around the green walls of the governor's reception hall. Two electric chandeliers overhead were doing nothing to disperse the gloom since the generator was not running.

After the predictable soften-up questions about the challenges facing his administration in Kuito, I asked the governor why the runway had not been repaired in two years. He did not even blink:

'Unfortunately, the company contracted to do the job did not have the technical capacity to complete the task.'

One of the humanitarian staff whispered later that Paulino dos Santos had been urging WFP to provide food for distribution by local NGOs as well as the better-known international humanitarian groups. It turned out that three such NGOs were registered in the name of members of the governor's family.

Back in Luanda the next day I sat at the dining room table at the Brandãos' house, watching some of the footage of the *deslocado* camps on a video camera I had borrowed to take with me on that trip. The girls started to bring in the procession of dishes that comprised lunch.

Anabela followed, shaking her head as she looked at the images on the video screen.

'It's hard to believe we're in the same country,' she said.

3

When the war ends, you'll go by car

It was an airlift that kept places like Kuito and Camacupa from complete starvation, but Luanda was no less dependent on air transport to keep its stomach full. Not that the people in the capital's apartment blocks and suburbs were in danger of malnutrition; rather, the varied diet of the urban middle classes could be sustained only with the help of imports. Toilet paper, cooking oil and starchy pasta were among the few items manufactured locally. On the street, the local fruit was good, but at 70 kwanzas for a pineapple – three dollars at the then prevailing exchange rate – it was a luxury. The vegetables grown on the city's sandy edges were generally stunted, shrivelled and wormy. By contrast, a stroll through a Luanda grocer's store could yield cheese, dried fish and mineral water from Portugal, fruit juice, beer and canned vegetables from South Africa, sweet biscuits from Brazil, yoghurt from France, all at prices more familiar to northern Europeans than to Africans.

For businessmen, dabbling in the import trade was a less risky venture than investing in local agriculture or food processing. Entrepreneurs seemed to be scouring the bargain basements of the world for surplus goods. At one point there was an outbreak of Coca-Cola cans with Arabic lettering, thanks to an oversupply in Algeria. Windhoek beer came and went in the course of a few months: Namibian Breweries were changing their label design and someone had found in Angola a ready market for the old stock.

Why make it locally when you can fly it in, was how the logic seemed to go.

Eventually, this principle established for tinned tomatoes was happily extended to elephants. In a country where road travel was so dangerous, air transport was applied to areas other than food imports – and it was army officers who had most of the planes at their disposal. So when a group of generals decided to create a wildlife park near Luanda, they didn't think twice about flying in animals from South Africa.

Maps of Angola show a sizeable proportion of the country as designated game reserve. The park boundaries have existed on paper since colonial times, but were rendered irrelevant during the years of war that followed independence. Wildlife became a ready source of food for soldiers who had guns but no pay packets. Now, the game reserve closest to Luanda – the Kissama National Park – had been earmarked as the spot for Angola's first elephant airlift. The park was being re-established under the auspices of a body called the Kissama Foundation. President dos Santos was the patron, and the list of trustees included a high proportion of FAA generals and the South African politician Roelf Meyer.

At 4:30 a.m. one Sunday morning, a selection of four-by-fours drew up in the car park outside the Angolan National Radio building. A convoy was assembling to drive down to Kissama and witness the arrival of the elephants. The man who seemed to be in charge wore game ranger's khaki and introduced himself, in a South African accent, as Filipe. Since his name and looks suggested Portuguese ancestry, I asked him how long he had been in the country.

'Since '92,' he said.

'Have you always worked in conservation?'

'No – I was a missionary – ha ha.'

After the 1992 elections, when UNITA went back to the bush and the government found itself wrong-footed with a much-diminished army, the Angolan government had called in mercenaries – specifically a South African firm named Executive Outcomes – to help it win back the territory that UNITA had grabbed. The Executive Outcomes men knew UNITA's methods very well, since many of them had been fighting in the South African Defence Force on the same side as UNITA, right up until the late 1980s. Now, having completed their tour of duty on the government side, they had found alternative employment as game rangers.

We headed out through the scrappy edges of Luanda in the dark, watching sparks from the cigarette ends that Filipe was throwing out of the window of the car in front. Dawn was already breaking as we crossed the big suspension bridge over the Kwanza River, which rises in the Central Highlands and passes close by Camacupa, taking a big arc through the country and forming the northern boundary of the Kissama park before emptying into the Atlantic. Within the limits of the game reserve lies the military airport of Cabo Ledo, conveniently situated for a wildlife transport operation that happened to be run by generals. Cabo Ledo was now the national headquarters of the Commandos – the FAA Special Forces. Back in 1992, when Executive Outcomes came to the rescue of the MPLA government, it was at Cabo Ledo that the South African mercenary force had based itself.

As we stood around the cold grey airfield waiting for the plane to arrive, it was evident that Filipe was not the only former missionary, ha ha, who had returned to his old haunt. Also in attendance were the Angolan generals who directed the project. A remarkable number of them were white. One theory current in Luanda posited this as part of a classic Dos Santos strategy: having whites in control of the army was a safeguard against a coup. Even if the generals wanted and managed to overthrow the president, they would not have the popular support to enable them to stay in power.

There was little incentive, in any case, for generals to stage a coup, considering how the Dos Santos presidency did nothing to prevent the military commanders from helping themselves to whatever army property happened to catch their eye. The vehicles painted in the livery of the Kissama Foundation all had FAA number plates, marking them as military assets. When the plane carrying the elephants rumbled into view and screamed along the runway, it was one of those pregnant-looking Russian transport aircraft leased by the FAA to move troops and military equipment around the country. Nor was it a problem that an American donor and his wife were arriving on the plane without the visas that normally take weeks to issue. One of the generals would be able to sort that out with immigration, and there would be no questions asked when they departed on a scheduled flight from Luanda airport.

As we watched, the containers with the elephants came sliding out of the cargo hatch at the back of the plane, elephant piss pouring from the bottom and, now and then, a trunk waving primaevally from the top. There was banging and shouting at the benign end of *confusão* as the containers were loaded onto flatbed trucks. We left soon after: a convoy of showroom four-by-fours with executives and guests, followed much more slowly by the trucks with the elephants. The sky was overcast and white, and the trunks of the baobabs and the euphorbias whiter still; it all looked like an image in negative. And those shapes: the baobabs, thick all the way up then dissipating into silly little branches, and the euphorbias, thin all the way up, then exploding into long angular fleshy leaves.

The convoy stopped at a crossroads in the bush and the trucks lumbered up. Everyone stood on top of vehicles as, one by one, the doors of the four containers were opened by former mercenaries in overalls standing on top of the container. Some elephants charged, others wriggled out. The last elephant, however, proved more difficult. Ominous thumping noises from inside the container provoked increasing consternation among the people in green overalls. The elephant had fallen over and the container was not roomy enough for the animal to get back onto its feet.

Solid metal was posed against solid flesh, and neither was going to give: it was what Angolans would call a *situação* (situation), not quite *confusão*, but a state of affairs beyond human agency that might well spin out of control and lead to *confusão*. When it proved impossible to pull the container to pieces, using a Land Rover and a crane mounted on one of the trucks, an attempt was made to hoist the elephant back onto its feet with cables attached to the vehicles.

The next plan involved administering a drug to the elephant and dragging it out bodily through an opening narrower than itself. When the laws of physics put paid to that plan and the mercenary warders were starting to look very worried indeed, the elephant suddenly jumped up of its own accord.

A month later there was a second airlift to Kissama. This time the containers that came off the plane were special tall ones. Giraffes. And the chaos began immediately. The one crane that was available did not seem equal to the task and, in a frenzy of snapping cables, it looked for a moment as if one of the containers was going to split open and spill giraffes all over the tarmac. But they got it onto the truck and we set off along the sandy track. A hatch had been opened on top of the container, and two giraffe heads bobbed along at baobab height until we got to the place where all the animals were to be released. It was not only giraffes: zebras streaked out, then ostriches waddled out fast as they do, and, finally, the giraffes. One wandered out placidly. The other charged out, then turned round and ignored us. Word came on the radio that the second truck had got stuck.

In the meantime, the generals and the general bystanders attacked the coolboxes of beer, whisky, pastries and sandwiches. Away from the picnic, a woman wailed in anger. Her son, a park employee, had been with the second convoy. As they had tried to free the trailer, it had collapsed, trapping him underneath and breaking both his legs.

A few weeks later, Rádio Ecclésia reported that a market near the park boundary had been offering braaied zebra.

While the generals kept busy with their pet conservation project, the war continued. News came in slowly of an attack on a passenger train near Zenza do Itombe, about 150 kilometres south-east of Luanda: the same line whose trains limped alongside the road to Viana and the *deslocado* camps there. First we heard that 16 people had been killed, then 100, and that the train had run over an anti-tank mine that had been placed on the track. Rádio

Ecclésia's correspondent in Ndalatando, the nearest provincial capital, declared that '*o clima de consternação é total*'. It seemed that the explosion had ignited fuel that was being transported, creating a fireball.

Some of the survivors had made it to Luanda's Josina Machel hospital, which stood at the summit of the hill between the city centre and Bairro Azul, its facade a faded version of the standard coral pink of government buildings. My first visit to the hospital went no further than the administrator's office. The administrator was not available, and without his *autorização* the guards were not going to let me into the hospital to speak to survivors of UNITA's attack on the passenger train. Next day the administrator was back at his desk, and a hospital orderly led me along the cloisters to a ward where a man in his fifties called Joaquim António was lying shrunken in the corner of his bed. He told me he had been travelling home from his nephew's funeral in Luanda when the train hit the mine and caught fire.

'I saw my life disappearing before me. Many people died. God helped me. Although my leg was broken, I was still able to get out of the window. There was fire around the carriage. If I had jumped the other side, I would have died, without a doubt.'

His voice, weak to start with; dropped to a husky whisper and died away.

'*Crianças moreram. Crianças, crinçasssssss.*' Children died – children, children.

Natália Manuel was 24 years old. She had caught the train to take vegetables to sell in the market in Dondo. She had taken her three-month-old baby with her.

'The train hit the mine, and stopped. Then the shooting (*tiro*) began, and the fire (*fogo*). *Fogo fogo fogo, tiro tiro. Fogo fogo, tiro tiro.* I managed to escape through the window with my baby. By the time we got to the road, I could no longer walk. But a man carried me on his back to the town. We were welcomed and well treated – but many, many people died.'

From Joffre Justino in Lisbon came the statement with UNITA's version of events: the train had been carrying soldiers and ammunition (and was by implication a legitimate military target). Joaquim António, Natália Manuel and her baby, however, were not soldiers.

✤

That weekend there was a march in Luanda to protest against the train attack. It was organised by the government since no one else was allowed to convene protest marches. But to whom could the protesters protest? Not to Savimbi, whose whereabouts were unknown. And not to the UNITA office in Luanda, since that was in the fiefdom of Eugénio Manuvakola, the man who had dissociated himself from Savimbi and founded a faction called UNITA-Renovada which the government conveniently regarded as the real UNITA.

The United Nations was thus chosen as the target of the march. But the compound that housed the UN's political division – the part whose job it was to stop the war – was some 20 kilometres out of town. So the destination for the procession became the 1960s block downtown where the UN Development Programme and UNICEF had their offices. The marchers assembled on Kinaxixi Square, a long traffic roundabout in central Luanda; it had been fenced off with corrugated iron for as long as I had been in the city, and was to remain that way for another year while the fountains on the central island were rebuilt. MPLA banners dominated the scene, but there were little clusters belonging to other political parties too, including UNITA-Renovada. The march shambled down the hill to the UN building, where Cândida Celeste, the minister for the family and the promotion of women, handed over a piece of paper to a group of men in suits who looked rather unsure about what they were meant to do with it.

However many the party banners, it was hard to see this as an outpouring of popular anger. Taking to the streets was a luxury denied those whose grievances were against the government. A few weeks after the protest against the train bombing, José Rasgadinho, chairman of the Boavista residents' committee, was arrested one Saturday morning while on his way to a meeting with the committee's lawyer, David Mendes. Since the courts were not in session over the weekend, and Monday was a public holiday, Rasgadinho spent three days in the police cells. When, on the Tuesday, he was eventually taken before a magistrate, the case was dismissed and he was released immediately. No warrant had been issued for his arrest; the plainclothes men who arrested him were from a municipal force which had no authority in the place where the arrest took place, and they had told him he was charged with 'aggression', an act that is not listed as a crime in the nineteenth-century penal code that Angola had inherited from Portugal.

Rasgadinho's arrest was typical of the way in which the servants of the state went about their business. Around the same time, Gilberto Neto, a promising young journalist from an independent weekly, was granted a bursary by the Reuters Foundation to attend a training course in London. When he presented his passport at Luanda airport, an official had told him he was not allowed to leave the country since there was a criminal charge against him.

The supposed charge against Gilberto dated back to 1999 when Rádio Ecclésia had rebroadcast a BBC interview with Jonas Savimbi. Police raided the radio station's offices, and arrested several journalists. Gilberto, however, had no connection with Rádio Ecclésia; his misdeed was to write a report for his newspaper, *Folha Oito*, about the raid on the Catholic broadcaster. The police then raided *Folha Oito* and arrested Gilberto and his editor, William Tonet. The charges were later dropped.

Two years on, this fact had not reached the emigration desk at Luanda airport.

It was early September, and the Benguela current was still bringing sparkling, icy water and the smell of kelp up from the Cape of Good Hope. A group of BBC executives was visiting from London, and we lunched together at one of the Ilha's restaurants, its tables just metres from the sea. They gave me a lift back to the city centre, and as we got to their hotel one of them received a phone call. A plane had hit the World Trade Center in New York – on the opposite shore of the same ocean we had been looking at minutes earlier. We got to a television and saw pictures of the explosion at the Pentagon, then a split screen image showing the twin towers as well as the Pentagon.

When I went home to prepare for a long-planned interview with Tony Bloomberg, country director of UNICEF, I found Hilda in the living room, staring at the news footage from New York and Washington with the rapt attention she normally reserved for the Cartoon Network. The UNICEF interview, as I should have anticipated, was never aired. It was to have been part of a package commissioned to coincide with a UN children's conference in New York the following week. No one was surprised when the conference was cancelled, and the package scrapped.

Nevertheless, Angola may have one of the few places in the world where the events in New York and Washington were simply another news story from afar during those last few months of 2001. Events such as the attack on the passenger train near Zenza do Itombe were a reminder of problems closer to home.

The Saturday after the attack I went down to the Cidade Baixa and had my hair cut in a barber's shop with big curvy, clanky chairs from which the chrome plating was flaking off like dandruff, the mirror was speckled and the plywood panelling warped. The swivel chairs were useful: the shop had no electricity and the barber would turn the chair so that the part of the customer's scalp he was working on always faced the daylight coming in through the open door. On this occasion, staff and customers were engaged in an earnest discussion about the attacks in America, but with a detached kind of fascination, similar to the way in which Angolans discuss the Portuguese football league.

Around the same time I discovered the Elinga Cultural Centre, also in the Baixa: A colonial building with holes in the roof and in the floors, along with two long elegant upstairs rooms for exhibitions or dance classes, and a large terrace with space for an outdoor theatre and a bar. The Elinga bar was where the Luanda arty crowd used to hang out: painters, photographers, sculptors, actors, Rastafarians, people dedicated to reggae, rap, blues, rock 'n roll, traditional Angolan drumming, or any combination of the above. In deference to world events, someone had invented a cocktail called a 'Bin Laden', comprising equal quantities of rum and tepid Fanta. One of the artists had put together a garish expressionist multimedia canvas and was debating whether to call it 'Bin Laden' or 'Zenza do Itombe'.

The image of the burning World Trade Center also featured on a pile of pamphlets with which Pedro and Ana arrived in Luanda. Pedro was a young relative of Sebastião, an Angolan-born Portuguese citizen; Ana was his Spanish wife. They were evangelical missionaries who lived in South Africa but now felt a calling to evangelise Angola. In between meetings at government offices trying to obtain Angolan citizenship, Pedro and Ana would walk the streets of Luanda, bestowing upon Angolans their tracts which depicted not only the World Trade Center, but nuclear bombs, supermarket bar-code scanners and other symptoms of millennial decay. God was their travel agent: through prayer they got free passage on a boat to Lobito and a discount on their flight back to Johannesburg.

Another family member who started making frequent visits to the house around the same time was Anabela's 92-year-old grandmother. She dressed in an African print wraparound skirt and the black headscarf and blouse of Portuguese widowhood and came originally from Ndalatando, not far from where UNITA had blown up the train. The old lady would have been around 40 years of age when Angola changed from a colony to an overseas province of Portugal, and was already of pensionable age at independence. Her voice was frail, but her eyes gleamed. The one assessment of 92 years of living in Angola that I managed to catch was: Angola is a whore *('Angola é uma puta')*; people come here, have their way with her, and leave.

September brought spring to Angola, and the jacaranda trees in Lubango gave an ultraviolet tinge to the sky above Angola's southernmost city. Not only the jacarandas, but also the sandstone mountains and the blond wheat fields were a reminder that, if Angola straddles the imaginary line between southern and central

Africa, Lubango is firmly in the south. It had been the first major city to fall to the invading South African army in 1975, but since then had largely been untouched by the war. The highlands to the north of the city were fiercely contested by UNITA and the FAA. But south and west of Lubango, where nomadic herders competed for land with big commercial farms, there was no hope for an army accustomed to feeding off peasant farmers. UNITA never gained a foothold.

The big farms in the region were the reason I had been invited to Lubango with the World Food Programme (WFP) and the then minister of social services, Albino Malungo: the government had purchased locally-grown grain and was now donating it to WFP. The handover ceremony in the grain warehouse thus afforded the bizarre spectacle of Ronald Sibanda, WFP's national director, offering profuse thanks to minister Malungo and to the government – for donating food to the people for whom Malungo's department was supposedly responsible in the first place. (No less surreal was Malungo's remark to me on the plane en route to Lubango. On hearing I was South African, he had opined – in reference to the farmers who had supplied the grain – that 'Angola ought to succeed because, like South Africa, Angola has white people who are dedicated to the country.')

Afterwards, the government and WFP delegations and journalists were all invited to lunch at the provincial governor's house, a big pink pile on the main square. Chivas Regal was sloshed around before we were handed the menu: four courses with two or three choices for each course, a banquet worthy of the World Food Programme indeed.

My interest lay more in getting out of the warehouse and seeing something of the south-western corner of the country. On the UN's security map, where most of the safe zones comprised a small ring around each provincial capital, the south-west caught the eye as an exception: the coastal province of Namibe and the adjoining western reaches of Huila and Cunene provinces were safe for a pastime rare in Angola – road travel, as attested by the Namibian- and even South African-registered cars on the streets of Lubango.

The resemblance to South Africa went further than the landscape. The next day I headed out of Lubango towards the coast on a road that climbed out of the valley, over the ridge with its statue of Jesus that overlooks the city, and down to a fertile highland plateau. White farmers drove bakkies with their black employees riding in the back. But for the fact that the farmers spoke Portuguese instead of Afrikaans and drank espresso instead of Ricoffy, we could have been in the Free State. (On later visits to Lubango I spoke to land activists working for the rights of local cattle herders, who told of generals and other well connected people staking fences across the land and claiming it as their own.)

The flat land was an interlude. Soon we reached the top of the escarpment, where the road plunged over the Serra de Leba pass, tapeworming its way back and forth as it made its way from the highlands – Lubango sits at an altitude of 1780 metres – to the coastal plain in the course of a few kilometres. About half-way down, the first baobabs appeared. At the foot of the mountain we were in thick bushveld, which in the course of another half-hour's driving gave way to sandy desert, spotted with the tuber-like stems and straggling leaves of welwitschia plants.

It was Saturday, and I was travelling with a group of expatriate NGO staff to a spot on the coast where Rafael, a white Angolan who worked for the WFP, had set up a beach camp: a thatched shelter, a collection of tents, and a caravan that was not going anywhere. He met us as we arrived, and on discovering my nationality, he explained: 'I used to have a fishing business and they broke everything.'

'Who broke everything?' I asked. I knew UNITA had attacked a lot of white-owned businesses after the elections, though I had not heard of any damage being done in this part of the country.

He waved a hand indicating his employees and went on conspiratorially: 'You need to beat them. But if you beat them you are called a racist.'

Red sand cliffs stretched slowly around a bay of cold blue water. Nothing else. I saw what I thought was a log on the beach until I got close and it mutated into a seal and flopped its way indignantly into the sea. Luanda seemed very far away.

Two days later I was again with Rafael, the campsite owner, in a restaurant in the town of Namibe. There were a lot of white people there, clearly locals, and I asked Rafael why there were so many whites in this part of Angola, why they did not all leave at independence as had been the case in Luanda.

'There has never been conflict between the races here,' he replied.

Namibe, with its streets of single storey nineteenth century buildings painted blue and pink and its harbour with rusted cranes dating from the 1930s, lay stranded between the desert and the sea. The restaurant where we ate comprised a thatched shelter, the tablemats advertising Castle Lager and the television showing Portuguese satellite channels. We learnt that, two days earlier, the United States and United Kingdom had begun bombing Afghanistan.

Back in Luanda, Angola's own war showed no signs of waning. In the course of a week, 12 000 people arrived at a camp outside Caxito, driven out of their villages in the region of Nambuangongo, 200 kilometres to the north. The drizzle that marks the coming of spring was falling, as people started to construct shelters on the damp green hillside. Many were doing so for the second time; they had left their homes and headed for the same site near Caxito when UNITA overran the country after the elections.

'We were here in '92,' one man recalled. 'But then the government said we could go back home. We were planting our fields, re-creating our lives again – now we have seen everything destroyed a second time.'

Three months had passed since the attack on the school, and Caxito was once again being seen as a safe place. Yet a few days later, UNITA managed to hit within Luanda city limits. Someone fired what appeared to be a rocket-propelled grenade into an electrical sub-station in Viana. Electricity black-outs were nothing unusual in Luanda, but the attack left the city without power for longer than normal.

'It is time for Angolans to say, "Enough is enough".'

The Archbishop of Lubango, Zacarias Kamwenho, was a quietly expansive man, alternately blinking at his notes through his thick glasses and beaming out at the world – rather like an Angolan Desmond Tutu. Dom Zacarias, to give him the royal title that the Portuguese language bestows on a bishop, was talking in the air-conditioned conference room of the Trópico Hotel. The church was launching a campaign for peace. Through it ran a theme that had been growing in volume among Luanda's intellectuals and religious leaders: that the government and UNITA continued to wage war despite their protestations of desiring peace; that neither side could be said to represent Angolans, since Angolans genuinely wanted peace; and that the reason the previous peace efforts had failed was that they took account of the views of two armed movements and not of the Angolan people.

The Bishop of Uige, Francisco de Mata Mourisca, rose to speak: lean, ascetic, white; a figure from an Italian mediaeval painting. He talked of the 'incomprehensible logic' of the government and UNITA. 'Not wanting to make war, yet making war; not wanting to kill, but ordering killings; not wanting there to be deaths, but causing deaths.'

The *Jornal de Angola* had its say the next day: 'Certain disciples of terrorism in Angola are not hesitating from using the house of God to whitewash their image.'

It was in Dom Francisco's own diocese, in the north, that the war struck next. I had been planning to go to Uige to do a run-of-the-mill story about a farming project for displaced people. Now something had happened worthy of real news – and precisely for that reason I was not able to go there, since the airport was closed. I sat at home for the next few days trying, via the bad phone lines to Uige, to piece together what had happened:

Three UNITA columns, estimated to number 1 000 soldiers in total, had arrived at three in the morning, one of them managing to set up mortar launchers on a hill well within the city limits. The columns had got as far as the city centre before being engaged in battle by the FAA, and retreating. The following morning, fighting was still going on around a displaced people's camp only four kilometres from the city centre.

Much later, Maria Flynn, the UN's humanitarian chief in Uige, told me that she had spent the night crouched behind a barricade of sandbags in a room in her house which UN security regulations had required her to prepare in case of such an event, keeping tabs by radio on other aid staff – most of whom were also trapped in their homes as fighting went on around them. The following day, she had supervised an evacuation of humanitarian personnel from the town. The airlift had been delayed by the immigration officials at the airport, who insisted on checking every passport and writing the details in an exercise book. It was only at that point that the state television station had sent in its reporters to get the government line on the situation.

'The TV team arrived on a plane – they kept the propellers running while they rushed into town,' Maria recalled. 'They found two people on the street to say "Uige is calm, nothing's happening". Then they dashed back to the airport and took off.'

Independence Day, 11 November, was one of the few occasions when Dos Santos addressed the nation. His description of Jonas Savimbi as 'a habitual loser' and his promise of an imminent military victory seemed like an optimistic assessment after the FAA had been wrong-footed in Uige. FAA statements, parroted by the state media, concentrated on the situation in the east, claiming that UNITA officers were surrendering. It was there, in the province of Moxico, where UNITA retained control of its last scraps of territory and where Savimbi was said to be hiding out, that the FAA appeared to be concentrating its efforts.

'*Quando a guerra acabar, vai no carro!*' When the war ends, you'll go by car!

Seven o'clock on an overcast summer morning at the military airport in Luanda; a soldier was chivvying one of the passengers who had bought her way onto an army transport plane. She and her fellow travellers shuffled out towards the Antonov, dragging or carrying their overstuffed parcels and carrier bags. In the corner of the waiting-shed, someone had now installed a television. We could watch the Brazilian chat-show *Mais Você*, presented by a peroxide blonde diva who occasionally exchanged banter with a green parrot puppet.

The WFP plane was bound for Luena, the capital of Moxico province. As we headed inland the clouds broke just for a moment, revealing a river curving through a green landscape, but by the time we approached Luena there was once more cloud above us and beneath us. I felt queasy as we descended, and only when we dropped out of the cloud did I realise why. The ground was on our right, the cloud was on our left: we had just spiralled through the vapour with no visual reference points to indicate that that was what we had been doing. The airport officials halted us with forms marked 'international arrivals' as though we had landed in a different country from Luanda.

The town was hidden damply under trees that were in full dark leaf and, at least along the main avenues, trimmed into regular shapes. The architecture comprised the usual candy-coloured concrete slabs. It showed none of the obvious war damage of Kuito, but if anything Luena seemed even more sullen.

Overhead, the groan of the army helicopters was so persistent that after a while one ceased to notice it. No elephants and grocery imports here; Moxico was where military aircraft were being put to their originally intended purpose, and the cargoes were human. The planes and helicopters heading out of town were most likely taking soldiers towards the operational zone, which could mean anywhere between Luena and the Zambian border, 500 kilometres further to the east. But those aircraft coming into town were filled with civilians. Now and then an army truck would rumble along the otherwise empty road, the back crammed with people being driven from the airport to the local office of the social services ministry. Other people who had walked into town also made their way, on bare feet, along the avenue to the social services office, a building that had had most of its windows bricked over or covered with zinc. There they huddled in a large, dark shed or tried to make fires in the muddy yard, before being allocated a place in one of the *deslocado* camps out of town.

That evening I sat at a table outside one of the town's two bars, drinking Castle Lager – the only brand available in Luena, since aluminium cans were easier to fly than the bottles produced by the Luanda breweries – with foreign aid workers; British, Dutch, Zimbabwean, Mozambican. Everyone was talking of a scorched earth strategy: the FAA, they said, was systematically evacuating the areas of the countryside where UNITA was in control. With no one to farm the land, there would be no food for UNITA's soldiers. The fact that there would be no food for anyone at all seemed to be of minor importance. The donors were supposed to look after that, and the humanitarian organisations were indeed battling to open new *deslocado* camps fast enough to keep up with the flow of people.

The *deslocados* were already starting to build houses in the Muachimbo camp, half an hour's drive out of town, which I visited the next day. They were using strips of bark to lash together the horizontal and vertical poles to make a solid frame on which to construct daub and wattle walls. Later, after the end of the war, I would learn that this technique was UNITA's trademark. But Muachimbo's newest arrivals were still living in the dirt, with only the UN's blue plastic sheeting between them and the rain. One woman was wrapped in a piece of cloth that covered little of her skeletal frame. Somehow, she was still managing to breastfeed a baby. Her husband told me simply that 'we came here with the government – there in the bush, there was too much suffering.'

Others protested that they had been brought to Luena against their will. 'The government forces captured me in the fields and brought me here,' explained a woman at Katepue, the next camp. 'I came in a helicopter – I didn't want to leave my home.'

Her family had remained behind: 'At first they must have thought I was dead, but when they didn't find my body they must have realised I'd been captured.'

That evening we watched *Titanic* on a video. I was staying at the house rented by GOAL, the Irish humanitarian organisation, hosted by Roque, an Angolan GOAL employee whose Grace Jones hairstyle was more typical of the Congo where he had spent much of his life. The video had Portuguese subtitles, which Roque read out loud for the benefit of the younger children. We were watching a film about a shipwreck, a thousand kilometres from the sea, and a lot further than that in terms of life experience. But one of Roque's friends explained: 'It's a love story. It's universal.'

❖

The Luena military barracks was easy to find, in the middle of town, but the top brass was nowhere to be seen. Their attention was required elsewhere: UNITA had just attacked Cazombo, near the Zambian border. Not far from the barracks was the railway station. The town had owed its existence to the Benguela Railway in its eastward thrust to the Congo. Vegetation now engulfed the trucks that stood by the platform, and the station building was blackened by the fires of those who had camped out there. During the 1990s, when UNITA advanced through the countryside and people fled into town, the station had been pressed into service as a refugee centre. So had the Museum of the Revolution, a monumental concrete block that had been a cinema, on the outskirts of town in the middle of cultivated plots. The grass was now growing high inside the building too. 'Museu da Revolução' was still painted on the pink exterior, but all that remained of the exhibits was a tank and the tail of a shot-down South African plane displayed outside.

Where the town ended, the minefields began, on the very edge of Luena: little red signs marked with a skull and crossbones, sprouting like flowers from a field just across the road from where people were growing maize. Mine victims accounted for a sizable proportion of the admissions to Luena hospital with its signs along the drafty, unlit corridors indicating *enfermeria cirúrgica* (surgical ward) or *enfermeria ortopédica*. Except that the signs abbreviated *enfermeria* to *enfer*. To anyone who knew French, it did look like surgical hell, orthopaedic hell. A hell with beds, admittedly, but no blankets and not much glass in the windows. Other wards were labelled *pé minas homens* and *pé minas mulhers* – mine-foot men and mine-foot women.

Bernado Kanguenge, I suppose, fitted into the category of mine-foot man. Staring blankly from his mattress, bandages round the stump of his thigh, he told his story with bureaucratic attention to detail:

'On Saturday morning, 10 November, my hut was falling down. So I went into the bush to cut sticks to repair it. I was walking on a narrow path, when I stepped on a mine. A man found me and brought me to hospital.'

In the hospital director's office, a blast of cold air from the air-conditioner welcomed me. Decorative tiles covered the walls; the office furniture seemed to have come straight from the showroom. Installed behind a mahogany desk, the director looked as though he would not want to enter one of the *enfermerias* for fear of dirtying his suit. Only two other buildings in the town showed such signs of renovators' attention, one a suburban villa with fresh paint, large picture windows and air-conditioning powered from a generator. It belonged to a general.

The other was the town's posh bar: Pastelaria/Steakhouse Viví. Tiles everywhere, waitresses in pastel-coloured uniforms, the *kizomba* music of the coast playing on the battery-operated stereo, Portuguese Sagres beer and South African Savanna cider and Castle Lager flown in on the military planes, some elderly pastries and doughnuts – it was trying hard to be a Luanda coffee shop. Things like La Vache Qui Rit cheese and packets of biscuits were ranged in glass cases in the manner of a Soviet grocery store.

Almost all the customers were officers in uniform.

4

Peace breaks out

Nothing ever happened in Luanda on a Friday evening. Nothing of concern to journalists, that is. Friday night is the favoured time for Angolan couples to get married, allowing for a whole weekend of post-nuptial celebrations. So, when the rifle fire snapped and the flares exploded over the *bairro* of Samba on that hot February night, it seemed as though the wedding feasts were simply a bit more boisterous than usual. My attention was concentrated on guiding the rickety Reuters Hyundai between potholes in near-total darkness after giving someone a lift home, the only light coming from paraffin lamps on the tables that people used as market stalls.

Out of the *bairro* and onto the main road, the traffic seemed to be moving faster than usual. People were screeching and singing through the windows of buses and minibuses. Military trucks roared along as well, soldiers having a party in the back. As I reached the airport roundabout, the car stalled. I managed to freewheel to the kerb without getting hit by a truck, and tried to start it again. Not a murmur from the engine.

The roundabout's central island, incidentally, was now surrounded by high corrugated zinc fencing. The fountains and statues – one of the few public works projects in Luanda that had been both new and well maintained – had disappeared to make way for something still newer and as yet mysterious.

It was then that my cellphone rang. Someone had heard a report on Angolan National Radio. Jonas Savimbi was dead.

I abandoned the car and took a *candongueiro*, a minibus taxi, to get home to the flat in town that I had been renting since the beginning of the year. After the gunfire in the *bairros*, the city was uncannily quiet for a Friday night. I had to start working, with not very much to work with. The army statement on the Angola Press Agency website said its soldiers had shot Savimbi in the bush in Moxico.

I had spent the previous nine months trying to cover a war at long range, despite the assumption from everyone who was not in Angola that since I was in Angola I was automatically in the thick of things. I had spoken to nuns. I had spoken to *deslocados*. I had spoken to diplomats and to aid workers. Now here I was, sitting with an allegation which, if true, would be the most important thing that had happened in the recent course of the war. And it seemed even more remote than anything that had preceded it. No independent confirmation, and little chance of getting any, considering that it was now 10:00 p.m., the event had happened more than a thousand kilometres away in a place where the phones did not function, and the only possible witnesses would have been soldiers.

In between the several calls that came through each hour from various BBC programmes and from the Reuters office in Johannesburg, I nipped downstairs to find out what the word was on the street. Hardly anyone was about. Beneath the drips of the ill-functioning air-conditioning units I buttonholed a few stray figures and did the journalistic thing of asking what they thought. The flares and chanting of the *bairros* seemed a long way away. In central Luanda's half-lit blocks of flats, ambivalence reigned.

Said one man: 'He wanted war, war all the time. It was always like that. It was all he aimed for. Peace will come.'

Another was sceptical: 'I've heard a lot of hearsay about this.' (He used a colourful word for 'hearsay' – '*boato*' – which was new to me.) But he was not happy about the thought of Savimbi being dead. 'He was the only real opposition leader, the only one who could really challenge the MPLA.'

It was late, and I went to bed wondering whether the new day would bring any positive proof that Savimbi was indeed dead. My first priority on waking, however, was a dead red Hyundai on the airport roundabout. At 6:00 a.m. I jumped on a *candongueiro* back to the airport and was half surprised to see the car still there, though it looked as though it had been tampered with. After a few tries, I got it started, but had not had time to pull away before two men in plain clothes flashed police identity cards at me. The car, they told me, had been reported stolen. I would have to come with them to the *esquadra* (that ominous Portuguese word for a police station, with its echoes of squads and squadrons) to redeem the car – even though this meant driving them to the station in the car since they had no vehicle.

I was back at my desk by the time London was waking up and wanting new news. But what? Savimbi was still, in news dialect, only 'reportedly' dead, and I was still more than a thousand kilometres from the reported body. The government media was saying the body would be shown to journalists later in the day. Journalists? Which journalists? I called Manuel Mwanza, the Agence France Presse correspondent. I could hear Mwanza's ironic smile in his voice: 'Independent journalists weren't invited.'

I kept an eye on the television. Early in the afternoon, the pictures came on: someone who looked very like Savimbi laid out on a table, his trousers round his thighs revealing vivid black and white striped underwear.

For an independent journalist seeing it through someone else's television camera, this was still one step away from confirmation. What was needed now was someone who knew Savimbi and who had seen the pictures to be able to confirm it was indeed he. That person turned out to be Joffre Justino, on the phone from Lisbon. 'Regrettably for our movement ...'

Savimbi was dead.

That, at least, was now a fact. There was still wild speculation about his body – the television had said it had been buried in Moxico, but rumours flew around Luanda that the corpse had been transported back to the capital lest UNITA members form a cult around his grave.

And as to the future, no one had any useful insights.

❖

Writing more than a year later, in an Angola where the death of Jonas Savimbi looks more like the start of a chapter than the end, it is hard to recapture the fear of that last week of February 2002. Some months after the event, I looked at an article I had written for the *Mail & Guardian*, which ran under the headline I had suggested to the sub-editors: 'Angola on a knife-edge'.

'There are warnings,' I had written, 'that Savimbi's death could further destabilise the country unless all parties make immediate and decisive moves towards peace.'

It was a fear born of the unknown, and anyone who could potentially have provided a clue as to what was going on was inconveniently – or perhaps conveniently – absent. On Sunday, President dos Santos flew to Washington for summit talks with American president George W Bush that had been scheduled months in advance. It was rumoured that the FAA had timed Savimbi's death to strengthen Dos Santos's hand at the White House, and that Dos Santos would take the opportunity call a cease-fire.

On Tuesday, I caught up with Mussagy Jeichande, the United Nations representative, who was going from meeting to meeting with the representatives of the 'Troika' (Portugal, Russia and the United States, the three countries the UN had put in charge of overseeing the Lusaka peace accord of 1994), and with Fernando da Piedade Dias dos Santos (alias Nandó), minister of the interior, who was running the country in the president's absence. Jeichande, a laconic Mozambican, said he was hoping for a cease-fire that might give UNITA 'time to think'. Yet Nandó, it seemed, was not in a position to decide on whether or not to cease hostilities.

That evening, I listened to Angolan National Radio broadcast a press conference live from Washington: a press conference with a president who was clearly unused to giving press conferences, particularly in a country with constitutionally guaranteed freedom of speech. An American journalist asked President dos Santos about press freedom in Angola. Dos Santos's thin, croaky voice is not equal to the task of expressing anger on radio, but it does self-righteous indignation rather well: 'We have five independent papers, and they are all very critical of me!'

Of a cease-fire was there not a mention. Any chance that Dos Santos might raise the issue then vanished completely as the president jetted off from Washington to Brazil. The Angolan state media reported a meeting with President Cardoso, but it was otherwise to be a 'private visit'. With Angola facing its most critical moment in recent history, the president had gone on holiday.

It seemed unlikely that there would be any decisive action coming from the government for a while. But finding out what UNITA was thinking was going to be even more difficult. We knew at least who Savimbi's successor was meant to be: UNITA had regulations for what happened when its leader died. By rule, the vice-president of the movement, António Dembo, would take over until such time as UNITA elected a new leader. The problem was that no one knew where Dembo was. No one in Luanda knew even whether he was alive or dead.

It was a fortnight before UNITA acknowledged that Dembo was, in fact, dead. More than a year later, his family were continuing to raise questions over his fate. In the absence of a body, let alone an autopsy, they had doubts over the official explanation according to which Savimbi's vice-president had died of diabetes, exacerbated by stress and hunger.

Meanwhile, a memorandum circulated to humanitarian staff spoke breathlessly of 'revenge attacks' by 'splinter groups' within UNITA that could lead in turn to reprisals from the FAA. It said army generals in the northern provinces of Malange and Uige had declared their intention to 'wipe out the enemy'.

Every three days, a violent rainstorm would turn Luanda's streets into tea-coloured rivers. Every five minutes, a *candongueiro* would go past my window, the stereo pumping out that summer's biggest *kizomba* hit, a bouncy electronic beat with the usual sentimental lyrics of thwarted passion: *sem o nosso amor* (without our love). From the government and from UNITA came not a word.

There was clearly not much point in hanging round Luanda. After spending nine months covering a war I could never get near, it seemed I was now trying to cover an outbreak of peace that I could not get near. I decided to do what I'd been doing all along – if you can't figure out what's happening on the battlefield, you can at least see the consequences. So I got onto a WFP flight back to Luena.

❖

Luena had gone very quiet. The helicopters were an occasional interruption now, rather than the incessant background noise they had been in December, which seemed like a very long three months ago. At the garrison headquarters, soldiers conducted a flag parade in driving rain, then hung around laughing and smoking in their waterproof ponchos.

In Pastelaria Viví, the uneaten pastries hardened under the counter, with only a few officers there now.

'My clientele will drop now the front is moving away', muttered the owner.

The front was moving to Uige, or so I was told during the course of a couple more crates of Castle Lager with the humanitarian community. It seemed that the FAA had its eye on the north of the country as the place where UNITA might keep going despite the loss of its leader. Uige province was, after all, the stamping ground of UNITA's General Apolo, the man who over the past year had managed to embarrass the FAA and the Angolan government time after time: the attacks on Uige city as well as the abduction of the children from Caxito nine months earlier.

The aid workers also told me about the Israelis. In January and February Luena had been full of Israelis operating electronic equipment that looked as though it might have had something to do with surveillance. They had been busy right up until the day Savimbi died. Then, in the words of one humanitarian staff member who also happened to be from the Middle East, 'they went away and left me all their falafel'.

One story going round Luena went like this: The Israeli ambassador had visited Luena towards the end of 2001. In the months before that, Savimbi had given several lengthy interviews by satellite phone to overseas radio stations. The ambassador had been amazed that the Angolans had been unable to trace Savimbi through his satphone, and offered to supply the technical help that they would need to do so.

On returning to Luanda I called the Israeli embassy to check whether this was true. I spoke to a political official who said he would check with the ambassador and get back to me the next day. He never got back to me. When I called him again, he said the ambassador had denied that the Israeli government had given any support to the FAA in tracking down Jonas Savimbi. American embassy staff – off the record, of course – had no doubt about Israeli involvement in Savimbi's death, though they could not specify to what extent the Jerusalem government or its embassy in Luanda had been responsible.

Numerous people have since asked what interest Israel might have had in offering such underhand assistance to Angola. The answer has, as always, to do with economic expediency: buttering up the business contacts. Tel Aviv is among the most important centres in the global diamond industry. Just as the Americans, with their eyes on Angolan oil, shipped in the grain that the MPLA then dished out under its own flag, so the Israelis needed to keep the authorities in Luanda on their side for when diamond contracts were quietly drafted.

Luena has two municipal cemeteries. One of them you can't miss: right next to the town centre, with crumbling marble tombs and a tall, rusting neo-gothic gate which looks worthy of Dracula when thrown into silhouette by the setting sun. Jonas Savimbi, however, was not in that cemetery.

The other graveyard appeared to have been built as an overflow to the first, on the edge of town near the minefields. Its graves are mass-produced, the resting places of settlers who died in the last two decades of the colony, unaware that the soil in which their bones lay would ever be anything other than Portuguese. This cemetery's main distinguishing feature was its one living resident: a Shakespearean madman dressed in brown rags, with a variety of crucifixes strung round his neck – one of them dangling to his knees, as big as a rifle. He asked me where I was from, and I told him South Africa.

'The capital of South Africa is Johannesburg, and Nairobi is a city in Uganda,' he informed me.

Over by the far wall was a rotund mound of red soil, under a tree. There was no gravestone. In the bark of the tree, someone had scratched the words 'Savimbi Jonas'.

It was the living members of UNITA, however, who were of more interest. I knew that the people who had arrived in Luena since Savimbi's death would have been the *bittereinders* – the people who stuck with the leader until the end. I wanted to know why they had held out for so long, and, for that matter, what they had been doing with UNITA in the first place. Were they devotees of Savimbi, or had they been abducted by the rebels and forced into a life on the march?

I got a lift to the Muacanheca displaced peoples' camp with a WFP driver who took his Landcruiser up to 120, 130 kilometres an hour. At that speed the idea seemed to be that you could sail over the waterlogged potholes rather than having to swerve around them. It was a good 20 kilometres to Muacanheca, a new settlement that had been hastily set up as the other camps around Luena became full. People crawled out from under the squares of plastic sheeting which had been all that had stood between them and the rain throughout the night.

Graça said she had been with UNITA for 18 years. This surprised me, because she barely looked 18. I asked her age.

'Twenty-four.'

'So you were six when you were captured by UNITA?'

'I wasn't captured by UNITA.'

This startled me. A six-year-old girl had joined UNITA of her own volition? Graça continued: 'UNITA sent me to study in Jamba in 1986.'

She had been taken from her home in Catabola – that forlorn place I had passed through between Kuito and Camacupa – to Jamba, Savimbi's bush capital in the far south-east. There, she said, there had been white people, 'South Africans and Americans, developing, reconstructing the country'.

'Back then things went well, Dr Savimbi was doing well', Graça continued. 'But when we got to 2000 and the offensive began, it got to a point where there was no food, no clothes, no medicines'.

My perceptions of UNITA had just taken a blow. Expecting to meet the gang of thugs sent by PW Botha and Ronald Reagan to crush the socialist aspirations of Angola's people, I had instead met petite young Graça, speaking the most fluent and the most articulate Portuguese I had ever heard in a refugee camp, and refusing to believe she had been kidnapped. She spoke of years on the move with UNITA until she came to 'the city'. She had 'never seen a city before'.

Graça was referring to somnolent Luena, with its broken shop windows and burnt-out railway station. She said she had been brought there after being captured by government troops, but added quickly, 'We were well looked after by the government, we were fine. When we got here to the refugee camp they gave us tents to sleep in'.

'If there were elections today, whom would you vote for?' I asked.

She looked shy, smiled, hesitated.

'If I could vote at this moment and there were many parties I would vote for President José Eduardo dos Santos because I prefer this life here'.

I threw her a stock question: 'Do you think there will be peace now?'

'We want peace, it would be welcome. We people have suffered hardships hoping that one day Angola would have peace and freedom – we will welcome peace sincerely and will be well disposed to it'.

'Do you want to go back to your village?'

'Yes, I want to go back to my village'.

'Do you think that will be possible?'

Again, she stopped short of answering the question outright.

'It would be best if it were possible for me to go back to my village, I'm willing. I want to get to know my family, I was small when I left, they won't even know me – my mother and father are dead but I will get to know the ones who are left, I want to go back to my village to say this is my grandfather, this is my cousin, this is my uncle.'

❖

Eduardo Paulo had joined UNITA when he was 20 years old. He was now 43, and looked closer to 60. It was 23 years since he had seen his home, in Chipeta in Bié province, where he had worked as a mechanic. The FAA had brought him in the previous day, in an aircraft from Luvuei – a place less than a hundred kilometres down the road from where Savimbi had died.

'People spent the whole rainy season without food, without salt, without medicines – so we came here to end that suffering. Children had health problems because of the lack of salt. So we said "Let's go over to the government".'

Knowingly or not, Eduardo had summed up the government's strategy. The deputy defence minister, Demostenes Chiwingutila – himself a member of UNITA's Renovada faction – had outlined new tactics against his one-time comrades in a speech to parliament that *Jornal de Angola* had quoted nearly two years earlier: 'The Armed Forces and the government have designed a strategy for the total destruction of the forces and means of Savimbi's terrorist organisation and this strategy follows certain objectives, one of which is the withdrawal of support for the people and organisation of Jonas Savimbi. Of course, these populations, after presenting themselves to the military, are directed to the centres for welcoming IDPs and, subsequently, the organs and institutions of the Government mandated for this, and the non-governmental organisations, give what help possible.'

Bluntly put, there was no need to shoot every peasant under the control of UNITA. It was enough to keep them on the run, to starve them out. The deputy defence minister had explicitly factored foreign aid into the government's military strategy.

Eduardo had lasted longer than most. His wife and one of his children had been captured the previous September, he told me.

'My wife is in Bié. I hope to meet my lady in Bié.'

'How do you know she is in Bié?'

'When I arrived here, the people from the social services ministry said, "Your wife is in Bié".'

Whenever Eduardo talked of peace, it was in the subjunctive mood, that verb form much beloved in Portuguese which emphasises the hypothetical nature of whatever is being talked about: '*Se haja paz*.' In the event that there might be peace.

Savimbi had failed to provide; now Eduardo's best hope for survival lay with the people whom he had learnt to see as his enemy.

'If there were elections in Angola now I would vote for the government as they are looking after me now.'

Back in town, people were still arriving on foot or in military trucks at the sodden yard behind the social services office.

Those who had clothes appeared to be dressed in uniform brown rags. Some of the new arrivals in Luena, however, were receiving marginally better treatment. These were the families of UNITA officers who were living in a house in the town, a building painted in the UN's blue and white livery that had once served as UNICEF's local office. The Children's Fund had moved on, and the children had moved in. A girl of nine or so was cooking *fuba* (maize meal) over a charcoal stove on the stoep. Another girl went inside the dim and unfurnished house to find the adults. Argentina and Adelaide were both in their fifties; both had the tired eyes of people who had seen too much.

Argentina had grown up in Kuito, and she seemed to have spent the last 26 years – exactly half her life – on the run. She had worked as a nurse with UNITA, studied in Namibia when it was South West Africa, worked in hospitals run by the South African military. It was difficult to imagine this gentle-eyed African lady collaborating with apartheid's invaders

Did she believe in UNITA's struggle, I asked her.

'In the beginning, yes, in '76. It was against the Cubans. But more lately we did not understand. When the American government imposed sanctions we became demoralised, lost almost all of our morale, because we had counted on the fact that with the help of the American government things would go well, there would be peace. But later people became worthless – the suffering increased.'

So the Cubans were the invaders from whom the white South Africans were liberators. Again, my preconceived notions of the war in Angola had just been inverted with chilling precision.

Argentina was the mother of ten children – 'nine living and one dead'. Her husband was a colonel in UNITA. She had stayed in Jamba until 1994 and ended up in Bailundo (one of the last UNITA-held municipal centres to fall to the FAA in the late 1990s) after the 1994 Lusaka accord. After several more years in the *mata* (the bush), she had arrived in Luena on 20 February, two days before Savimbi had died.

'Why did you decide to leave the *mata* after so long?' I asked.

'No one ever wanted to go to the *mata* in the first place,' she pointed out, showing a barely perceptible impatience for the first time in our conversation.'

'But why did you decided to leave now rather than previously?'

'Because we were captured. Before that we believed in the politics that had been inculcated – that the MPLA would kill us.'

Moments earlier, Argentina had been talking about being 'received very well'. There seemed to be a contradiction here. In what sense then had she been captured? Was it simply the case that after decades of seeing the Angolan government as the enemy, crossing into government territory could only be countenanced if it were a capture? Did Argentina and the other people with her have any choice? With UNITA's army all but wiped out, and UNITA's lands emptied of their farmers, it seemed that there was no option other than to go quietly with the government soldiers to the towns where they would at least receive food and shelter. Her husband had arrived in Luena with her, and was now at the military barracks. She did not talk of his being imprisoned at the barracks, but it seemed clear he and his fellow officers were not at liberty to join their wives and children in the house that had been set aside for them.

Captive or not?

Joining UNITA in the first place had, similarly, not been a matter of choice. Argentina's friend Adelaide recalled that for people living on the Planalto at the time of independence in the 1970s, 'there was only UNITA – that's how I joined UNITA.' She had spent the 1980s living with relatives in Huambo and had worked as a teacher at a school run by the MPLA government while her husband fought for UNITA. Reunited with her husband after the 1991 peace agreement, she had fled with him to the bush when Savimbi took his men back to war after the 1992 elections.

The following year she was back in Huambo as UNITA and the government battled for 55 days for control of the Planalto's largest city. When the government eventually expelled UNITA from Huambo, Adelaide and her family had fled back to the bush for a further eight years.

'In the *mata* one never had a fixed location, we were always on the move, and one day while we were on the move we were stopped by the FAA. They started shooting into the air – and we stopped.'

Thus had she come to Luena.

I asked her what she would like to do next.

'In the future ...' she pondered. 'While I was in Huambo I did a course in cooking and pastry-making. If the conditions existed for me to have a pastry shop in future, I would do that.'

Back in Luanda, I had barely unpacked my bags when the army announced that it had begun talks with UNITA in Luena. I wondered whether it was worth flying east once more. I knew I could wait days to get a flight to Luena, and by then it might all be over. I knew equally that I could get to Luena and still be barred from any useful sources of information, as well as being cut off from the internet and phone line in Luanda that kept me in touch with the rest of the world.

The state radio and television reproduced army statements saying that the talks were proceeding 'in a climate of brotherhood and understanding', while UNITA's Lisbon office insisted that the UNITA officers negotiating in Luena had been captured and forced to participate in the talks. In the lobby of the Trópico Hotel, I ran into the UNITA parliamentarian Jaka Jamba and asked him if he thought his comrades were indeed talking in leg-irons. His answer was convincingly ambivalent: 'They are not in prison, but they do not have freedom of movement.'

It was a comment that applied to the rain-soaked peasants and to the weary officers' wives I had met in Luena, as well as to the generals at the peace talks. For Jaka Jamba and his parliamentary colleagues in Luanda, as well as UNITA's officials in Lisbon and Paris and Rome, it must have been alarming to see the party's future decided by a group of people whose status as interlocutors depended on having staggered out of the bush and into the arms of their enemies at a particular moment in history.

'UNITA should be allowed to choose its own delegation at the talks,' Jamba muttered.

On Friday, Good Friday, a phone call from the government centre put an end to my deliberations about whether or not to return to Luena.

'There is a trip for journalists to Luena tomorrow morning. Be at the military airport at six.'

The smell of iodine rose from the tarmac as we scrunched across salt spilt from WFP stocks towards an Antonov, one of those lumbering juggernauts of the sky with a bumper-sticker saying 'Russia' on the door. The military authorities had been more generous with the guest list than was the case when Savimbi had died, five weeks earlier. Manuel Mwanza was there this time, as well as journalists from the independent Angolan weeklies, in addition to the generous handful from the state radio, television and newspaper. There were also some faces I didn't recognise: the young Brazilians from the company contracted to produce *Nação Coragem*, the government's multi-million dollar television propaganda slot.

Forty people inside an Antonov generate a lot of heat and sweat. As we started taxiing, the Russian co-pilot in his dungarees, sandals and yellow socks shuffled out of the cockpit and opened and banged the passenger door. This didn't stop something looking dangerously similar to smoke seeping in through the cracks as we were airborne. Just condensation of course, but the mood of the last few weeks had left open the possibility of anything and everything going wrong.

Much of the day in Luena was spent waiting. At the airport, the helicopters were lined up neatly at the far end of the apron. Another Russian plane ambled in, one of those planes that had been bringing in hundreds of people rounded up in the bush. This time, only three civilians shuffled down the cargo ramp: a bent old woman, a tiny child and a skeletal adult man, the war's last stragglers.

We piled into army bakkies and television jeeps and went to the provincial government buildings in town, where the Brazilian boys from *Nação Coragem* were all big hugs with the army generals. We hung round on the pavement – this was a part of Luena I had never seen: the fussy and torpid administrative quarter that seemed to have nothing in common with the decaying town. Across the square, a sign with the slogan: 'José Eduardo dos Santos – a leader worthy of a heroic people'.

No one was letting us into the building. Word went round that the FAA and UNITA generals had agreed on the text of a ceasefire plan, but the signing had been delayed by the absence of General Gato, who was to be helicoptered in from some indeterminate spot in the bush of Moxico. The absence of the political big man was worryingly similar to what had happened with the Lusaka Accord. In 1994, Savimbi had declined to sign that agreement in person, sending Eugénio Manuvakola as his envoy.

When, at last, the helicopter that was to have brought Gato landed, it was not Gato who arrived but a tall, sinewy, wild-eyed septuagenarian looking as though he had just landed from another universe – General Samuel Chiwale, the man who had been Savimbi's first military commander-in-chief. Gato, he said, had been too busy. So it was to be a signing without Gato after all.

We followed Chiwale into the conference room. At one end, crudely painted murals of Agostinho Neto and a Dos Santos who looked barely out of his teens gazed along the table – hardly neutral territory. The two military delegations looked ill-matched too, the UNITA officers shrunken inside fatigues that were far too big for them. The most emaciated of the lot was the man in the middle: General Kamorteiro, Savimbi's military commander-in-chief. Opposite him sat the leader of the FAA delegation, deputy commander-in-chief General Nunda. They worked their way through sheaves of papers, then stood up and embraced to an electric storm of camera flashes. Tiny Kamorteiro almost disappeared in the bear hug of the tall and muscular Nunda.

The war was over.

A reconciliation between enemies? In fact, the unequal hug was more like a reconciliation between estranged friends. Nunda was one of the UNITA generals who had gone over to the FAA during the 1990s; he and Kamorteiro had spent longer fighting alongside each other than against each other. The FAA's chief of staff, General Armando da Cruz Neto, the man credited with effecting the scorched-earth tactics that the FAA used to hound out Savimbi, was noticeably absent from the signing. There was undoubtedly a certain symbolic value in saving the big guy for the ceremonial signing which was to take place in Luanda the following week. But there was also a strategic benefit in bringing Kamorteiro face to face with his old comrade Nunda, rather than with Cruz Neto, whose light complexion made him the model of the old-style MPLA military man.

The signing over, the journalists mobbed a slight man in a pale grey suit which, like his colleagues' military uniforms, looked way too big for him. It was UNITA's information secretary, Marcial Dachala. With a certain feeling of awe, I put my first ever questions to a real live Savimbi henchman. Dachala listened patiently and spoke placidly as one journalist after another piled on the questions, the slightest tensing of his facial muscles the only sign that he was exhausted. I asked about the reports that UNITA's men had been taken prisoner and forced to enter into talks. He politely pointed out that the UNITA representatives in Europe had been mistaken:

'I think they were the victims on the one hand of distance, and on the other hand of problems with communications, but above all they were poisoned by certain media reports. Now they are in perfect concordance with what we are doing.'

I asked Chris Dell, the American ambassador, why the diplomats thought the peace agreement would work this time: 'I think the best guarantee this time is the fact that this is not something that either side feels has been imposed, or are being brought to the table against their will,' he said.

'It's obvious from the spirit we've seen here and the way this is evolving that this is something that comes from within the Angolans themselves.'

The reason the earlier peace efforts had failed so spectacularly was not hard to see: foreign governments, flushed with excitement by the end of the Cold War, had failed to realise that the Angolan war had a momentum of its own, and that in 1991 the two sides had been in no mood for reconciliation. Dell's assessment of the Luena talks was repeated often in the months that followed as all sorts of people praised a genuinely Angolan initiative. They ought to have said an Angolan *government* initiative − but that fact seemed to make surprisingly little difference.

A peace accord, or a surrender? The government knew it had won, but had the good sense not to gloat. UNITA would not admit it had lost, but its officers cannot have failed to realise that they would have followed their leader to his pauper's grave if they had not got a square meal very soon. And it was the government that held the meal tickets.

Five days later, on Thursday 4 April, I observed the UNITA generals, still in ill-fitting clothing, help themselves to the breakfast buffet at the Trópico Hotel before going to the signing of the cease-fire agreement. They barely looked strong enough to carry the plates of bacon, eggs and cheese, the plates of custard pastries and croissants, back to their table. I watched this as I drank coffee with Anita Coulson, who was visiting from London to conduct a journalists' training course. Anita had been the BBC correspondent in Luanda during the 1992 elections. 'You know what's different this time?' she said. 'They didn't bring their bodyguards with them.'

Anita could remember when those bodyguards became the Luanda vanguard of a UNITA army that remained largely intact. The puny UN peacekeeping force had been able to do little other than watch as UNITA handed in obsolete weapons and pretended to demobilise elderly men, or simply ignored its undertakings to disarm.

What followed was a decade of war.

❖

Angolan speeches invariably begin with a ten-minute salutation that mentions every single dignitary by his or her lengthy official title and equally lengthy multi-barrelled Portuguese name. The more solemn the occasion, the longer the roll call. So the signing ceremony at the National Assembly, intended to consign a war to history, meant the recitation of a veritable telephone directory at the start of each speech.

When Cruz Neto's own turn came to speak, he praised Dos Santos as 'the architect of peace'. The president, who had been out of the country for the fortnight following Savimbi's death, now sat centre stage, overlooking the signing as though he were the judge rather than a party to the dispute. General Gato, UNITA's interim leader, had to be content with a seat in the audience while Kamorteiro, the UNITA commander-in-chief, sat opposite Cruz Neto for the signing. Archbishop Kamwenho, who more than anyone else was the figurehead of the movement for a negotiated peace, was noticeably absent, lying low in Lubango, recuperating from an illness.

❖

Gunfire at a peace rally cannot be a good sign. All the assurances that the peace accord would hold this time round seemed to come to nothing as I heard the crackle of rifles. First I remembered my journalist's hostile environments training and prepared to hit the deck – and then realised that had I done so, I would have been trampled to death. So I joined the stampede.

The peace rally that took place the day after the signing ceremony was organised by the wonderfully-named National Spontaneous Movement: the state-sponsored rent-a-crowd which had come into being at a time when Dos Santos's popularity was flagging amid hyperinflation and ongoing war in the late 1990s. Advertisements in the press and on radio urged people to dress in white for the 'reunion of all Angola's children'.

And the people had turned out: Children in the white overcoats that Angolan pupils wear to class, people with white sheets wrapped round their heads, people holding white balloons; those who had cars driving them, with white fabric streaming from the radio aerial. The procession set off from the soccer stadium. There was a bus with its chassis almost dragging along the tarmac under the weight it was carrying, a crush of people oozing out of its windows and a whole lot more standing on the roof waving white bed linen and tree branches.

The end point of the march was the open ground near the MPLA headquarters, and at times the event looked like the ruling party's first rally for an election that was yet to be announced. MPLA banners were everywhere, and so were the T-shirts with a picture of Dos Santos and the words *Força Presidente* (Good luck, President). There were other party T-shirts there too, though no obvious UNITA presence.

A stout woman in a church group declared her neutrality: 'We are here not as politicians, but as patriots. We're wearing white to symbolise peace and the tremendous happiness we are feeling now.'

'Now the citizens who are in Luanda at the moment can get to know the 18 provinces of Angola,' chimed in a young migrant from Malange, daring to imagine the possibility of travel.

A dozen or so noisy youths were marching around chanting a slogan that translated as: 'Savimbi's penis got left behind in the bush.' But when they crowded around to shout their bit into my microphone, it became clear that if the government wanted to hijack the rally to its own ends it still had a long way to go.

'We want the government to deliver more money for schools!' the boys yelled. 'The government is corrupt! The government has been spending too much money on weapons!'

It was then that the gunshots crackled across the large empty lot, and we all ran. It was a false alarm. The gunfire was the work of some trigger-happy policemen shooting into the air to discourage people from stealing the crates of drinks that are an essential ingredient of any event organised by the National Spontaneous Movement.

The real damage was done on the other side of town from the rally. A crowd had spontaneously broken away from the main event, and spontaneously ransacked the Angonave workers' demonstration, which had by now been going on for well over a year.

By the following Monday, the strikers had returned, but their demonstration was now just a matter of forlorn-looking men standing outside a building. Their landmark posters had been ripped to pieces by the supporters of the same MPLA that had once called itself the Workers' Party.

5

I will soon be privileged enough to meet my family

Carlos looked like a child in fancy dress, the babyish face and pre-adolescent voice comically at odds with the camouflage gear that he was wearing. Carlos was not in fancy dress though. He had already served in battle during his two years in the Angolan Armed Forces (FAA). He said he was 13 years old. This was just about credible, but only because poor nutrition in early childhood makes many Angolan children appear younger than they really are. He looked closer to 11.

Carlos was playing with other children, clambering and swinging on the gun barrel of an abandoned tank in the middle of the main street in Cuemba.

What was he doing in the army, I asked.

'I joined the FAA because of the war.'

Knowing that I was speaking to a soldier, I tried to remember to use the polite, third person, form of address which in Portuguese is appropriate for addressing an adult whom one does not know personally. It was an effort not to slip into the familiar '*tu*' form which is used with children as well among friends.

Carlos had fought at Lungue Bungo, near Luena, in 2000: a battle that had given the FAA an important victory over UNITA. His answers were prompt but terse, like those of a pupil trying to please the teacher, as I tried to find out what went through a child's mind while engaged in armed combat.

'Were you afraid?'

'Yes.'

'What happened during the battle?'

'Deaths – injuries.'

'You saw all this yourself?' (I could not help slipping into the '*tu*' form now.)

'Yes.'

He did not know his family name, but knew that his father's name was Francisco António, and that his family were in Andulo, a place several hundred kilometres away on the other side of Bié province.

The future? 'I want to stay in the army,' he said, before declaring a moment later: 'I want to study.' He added that he had never been to school before, though someone had taught him to read.

There was only one question that caused him to hesitate.

'Do you think it's right for children to be soldiers?'

'I don't know. That's war.'

❖

Carlos's family was one among the millions of people whose movement from town to town and province to province had defined the last 10 years of the war in Angola. The war was over, but people continued moving. Those who had fled across the borders into Zambia and the Democratic Republic of Congo, some of them 20 years ago or more, were now coming back to places like Cazombo on Angola's eastern edge.

UNITA's soldiers and their families were still on the move as well: the agreement signed in Luena obliged UNITA to assemble its people – 55 000 soldiers in addition to their families, according to the memorandum – in 35 designated quartering areas scattered around the country.

The United Nations security map of Angola had developed a new outbreak of spots; the green zones that had previously surrounded only the provincial capitals now spread to the smaller towns where, in the last years of the war, the government had maintained only a tenuous grip and the aid agencies had not dared to venture. One such place was Cuemba, which had held a morbid fascination ever since those first visits to Kuito and Camacupa a year earlier; many of the people I had spoken to in the feeding centres at those two towns had arrived from Cuemba in search of food. With the war now over, the World Food Programme had started distributing rations there, and had invited along a group of journalists to go and look at what it was doing.

'We'll show you the waterfall,' the pilot said as we descended, and we swooped over the place where a wide river plunged and foamed into a gorge that sliced unexpectedly through the dry, pinkish grassland. The plane churned up orange dust clouds as we touched down on the earth runway, next to a crumpled Antonov that had crashed and come to rest near some banana trees.

At Cuemba we were housed in the *palácio*: literally, the palace, the title given to the official residence not only of a provincial governor, but of any municipal administrator of the status of a mayor. This *palácio* had no windows left, and most of the window apertures had been filled in with mud bricks to keep out the cold. A leopard skin with two bullet holes hung on one of the interior walls, which had been recently painted in deep green. The exterior of the building was the standard government pink. On the building opposite the *palácio*, someone had tried to paint over a sign, but the letters were still legible: UNITA Municipal Delegation.

The FAA had recaptured Cuemba in 2000 – the official version of history had it that civil administration had been restored in 2001. What 'civil administration' meant was the presence of an administrator – in this case one with a taste for designer labels (Polo jeans and a Nike swoosh on his baseball cap) – in a dilapidated *palácio*. There were not many signs of the administration doing anything more energetic than simply existing.

According to Médecins sans Frontières (MSF), which had sent a team to the town a few weeks earlier, one child out of every thousand was dying each day in the Cuemba area: 10 times the death rate that the statisticians of famine consider to constitute an emergency. The hospital facilities at Cuemba comprised about half a dozen metal beds. None of them had mattresses, so the patients – all of them children – sat on the cement floor or lay down if they were too weak to sit. In one corner a little girl coughed under the only blanket. No one reacted, or even focussed, as we entered.

It was the army that provided the few signs of activity in the town, which was home to the FAA's 20th Garrison. The soldiers were well clothed and looked well fed. A group of them were in charge of the *lancheonete*, a term that had become a dainty euphemism for some of the roughest-looking drinking holes in rural Angola. A military-issue solar electric panel was propped up against a tree, charging the car battery that would power the lights and the hi-fi for a few hours that evening. Soldiers also seemed to rule the town's small market. Broken bridges meant that Cuemba was still isolated from the world outside and the military planes were the only way to get anything in.

At the edge of the town, however, some of the administrator's functionaries were at work. In dusty ground beside a spiky concrete church and a scarlet poinsettia tree, employees of the government were writing down the names of the latest group of people to arrive in town, and issuing them with cards that would entitle them to receive food rations from the WFP.

A teenage girl wearily held up a pointy-eared rodent that she had caught to eat.

'There's nothing else to eat. I've eaten rats many times before.'

I asked her why she had been living in the *mata*. While she hesitated, a man behind her said impatiently 'UNITA burnt our fields'.

Rats were a rare source of protein. 'There were only sweet potatoes – a tiny, tiny, tiny bit for each person,' according to Aurélio, a white-haired old man who looked as though he had been pared down to his last sinew. He had been in the *mata* for eight years, 'because of Savimbi'.

Did he lose family members?

His response was chilling in its understatement:

'Only three members of my family died from hunger.'

In the queue for ration cards, a man named Evaristo told me that people had 'come for WFP's service, bringing food to the people of Cuemba'. He had come to Cuemba because 'now the government has managed to give food to the people.'

The government? The only conclusion to be drawn was that he thought the WFP was an agency of the Angolan government. It was an understandable mistake for a peasant farmer whose experience of a functioning state was no greater than his knowledge of the United Nations. The government-issued ration cards did nothing to dispel the impression that the food was a gift from Luanda rather than from foreign donors.

The sun set before six. It seemed like the dead of night when, at eight o'clock, Marcelo Spina Hering, WFP's information officer, helped me set up a satellite phone on the roof of a car so I could send a report to London. As we tried one angle after another, a man approached out of the darkness. He asked if we were interested in *pedra* – stones. We both declined. Marcelo, a Brazilian, confessed afterwards to being taken aback. Apparently, if someone offers you *pedra* on the streets of São Paulo, they will be trying to sell you not diamonds, but crack.

The only trucks in Cuemba belonged to the FAA. So it was on an FAA truck that the WFP team took the journalists to see the village of Chindumba, and a less hardy vehicle would probably not have survived the 30 kilometres of twisting sand track. Gilberto Neto, a journalist from the Luanda weekly *Folha Oito*, tied a bandanna round his face. Later I read his account of the journey: '... journalists breathing more dust than air, travelling through a forest of the kind that you see in films, where bandits are ready to jump out at you' – the place was as wild and strange to a *Luandense* as it was to me.

As the crow flies, Chindumba is only 18 kilometres from Cuemba, but blown bridges made the roundabout route necessary. Children yelled and cheered as the truck pulled into the village. The noise faded when they realised there was no food on board.

It was hard to move beyond the cliché of 'skin and bone' to describe the children and the mothers who had spent years in the *mata*. Donisa João was born in Chindumba. She had fled into the *mata*, surviving on leaves and roots, hunger eventually driving her to Cuemba where she spent a year. She had returned to Chindumba because there was no food in Cuemba either. Her husband had died a long time ago; her eldest son was in the *tropa*, the troops. Donisa did not specify which *tropa*. He could have been forced into battle either by UNITA or by the FAA, with no prospects of ever coming home again.

In one corner of the village, brick buildings had crumbled, and pawpaw trees had sprouted among their foundations. The bricks were stamped with the name of a company in Silva Porto – Kuito, as it has been called since 1975.

I asked one of the Angolan WFP staff what had brought Chindumba to what it was.

'Most of the people fled to the bush,' he explained. 'In the bush they could not cultivate – or if they could, any soldier could come from UNITA or the government side and get their food by force.'

I was reminded of a recent interview with Erwin van der Borgt, the country director of MSF-Belgium, who had returned from Cuemba shortly before my visit. Van der Borgt, calm and soft-spoken, was not a medical man but an economist by training, and he had coolly analysed the causes of the Angolan famine in terms of political strategy.

'Although the area has been under control of the government, hardly any assistance was being provided to the population,' Van der Borgt had said. 'Civilian populations were the target of both parties to the conflict – the government troops had an interest to force civilians to leave rural areas and take them to areas under their control. UNITA, from their side, had an interest in keeping control over those populations as well, but they were continuously on the run in the bush and they often forced those people to follow them. They were not able to settle, they were not able to cultivate.'

As in Luena, what I was seeing was the practical outcome of the strategy that the deputy defence minister's speech had put to parliament: 'The withdrawal of support for the people and organisation of Jonas Savimbi. Of course, these populations, after presenting themselves to the military, are directed to the centres for welcoming IDPs and, subsequently, the organs and institutions of the government mandated for this, and the non-governmental organisations, give what help possible.'

This succinct analysis of the famine – relayed in an article I wrote about Cuemba for BBC News Online after returning to Luanda – earned me my first meeting with Aldemiro Vaz de Conceição, the presidential spokesman. In any other country, a journalist could expect to be in daily contact with a presidential spokesman. But in Angola, the spokesman mostly remained aloof from the common mob that was the press. Rather, he would issue statements in the name of the president whenever it was deemed appropriate. So when I received a call from Vaz de Conceição's assistant, saying the spokesman himself would like to see me, I was delighted, expecting a rare interview opportunity.

On the appointed day I found my way to the State Protocol building, a colonial villa on top of the hill, adjoining the presidential palace, where I was led into a waiting room with heavy curtains, artificial flowers and fierce air-conditioning. Eventually, I was summoned into the presence of Aldemiro Vaz de Conceição, a picture of long-limbed elegance in gold-rimmed glasses and a suit that looked expensive. He had no intention of granting an interview. Waving a print-out of my article he asked me how I could have blamed the government. His wide-eyed surprise seemed as exquisitely composed as his outfit.

A traffic roundabout in the middle of the forest was the first sign that UNITA had been at work. There was not much traffic to use it; on the 40 kilometres of dirt track from Cazombo, the MSF bakkie had not passed a single other vehicle. Cazombo lies at the centre of the little block of territory that juts out between Zambia and the Democratic Republic of Congo, in the extreme east of Angola. The road out of the town took us towards the Zambian border, through stretches of bush, though grass-covered river flood plains, and finally though dense woodlands. Then a gateway, made of wooden poles and easily three metres high, appeared at the edge of the road where a smaller track entered the forest to our right. The track looked as though it had been hacked out of the forest only recently, and was marked on either side with stakes that had been charred into black and white bands, and driven into the ground. Then there was the lonely roundabout, with more stakes marking off the edge of the road and the central island. We saw barely a soul until the road led us to a wide clearing, with a *jango* (a thatched meeting hall) in the centre. We had arrived in UNITA territory.

Calala was one of the quartering areas where the April peace agreement had ordered the UNITA troops and their families to assemble in time for the September deadline. After that, a token contingent of 5 000 UNITA troops would be received into the FAA. The rest would be demobilised, receive whatever training and material support they needed to make a fresh start in civilian life, and be taken back to their home towns and villages.

That was the theory, at any rate. Demobilisation plans were later to descend into near chaos, with the number of people turning out to be twice what had been anticipated; for now, in June, UNITA officers were complaining that their followers were starving to death. UNITA, having chosen to site its quartering areas in remote corners of a country where internal transport had all but come to a halt, was now starting to realise that the FAA was not going to be able to magic up the food needed by over 100 000 people.

For a curious journalist, the quartering areas represented an excellent opportunity to put a face to the UNITA whose name had inspired such awe in Luanda, an awe deepened by the dread of something unseen, unknown, and stirred into demonhood by the government and its press. In a sense, of course, I had been meeting UNITA people ever since my first trip to Kuito, a year earlier. At that stage, though, none of the people who had limped into the government-controlled towns would admit to having been part of the rebel movement.

Later, in Luena, I had spoken to the people who had surrounded Savimbi almost until the end. But here in Calala, I finally came face to face with people who had never made a personal act of surrender. They had stopped fighting because General Kamorteiro, the emaciated man at the peace talks, had told them to stop fighting. Their laying down of arms was contingent on their loyalty to UNITA.

Apart from a small FAA detail in each camp to supervise the disarmament process, quartering areas like Calala remained under the control of UNITA officers. At first sight, the people could have been in a village anywhere in Africa: the boys playing soccer in a sandy lot, the girls walking silently through the forest carrying water containers on their heads, all of them looking reasonably well fed. UNITA's welfare official was a woman in a shiny scarlet dress and an impossibly elaborate plaited hairdo.

'Where did you to get your hair done?' I asked.

'There are people here who can do this,' she said.

What distinguished the quartering area from a normal African village was the meticulous planning in this settlement that had taken shape in the two months since the peace accord was signed. The roads were the most obvious sign, the side streets leading off to neatly arranged sub-villages. Most of the houses were complete; at others, people worked at tying poles together with strips of bark to make the frames or, at a later stage of construction, using handfuls of grass to thatch the roof. It was a self-made community: the sort of thing, perhaps, that in perverted form featured in the government's plans for the Boavista residents, who were offered a pile of cement and a site in the middle of nowhere and expected to get on with it. Someone had failed to realise that what worked for a guerrilla army did not work for a group of city-dwellers who had already constructed their homes, only to see them destroyed.

In the clearing opposite the *jango* was a set of buildings meant for administration, which stood empty most of the time. Tacked to the grass wall, a hand-written notice headed 'Government of the Republic of Angola – Quartering Area of Calala' informed residents how they could use the services of the International Committee of the Red Cross to trace lost relatives.

There was a hospital in the quartering area. I asked to see it, and was told to come in an hour. A surgeon in white mask and green theatre gown received me and took me through the grass house with its designated areas: waiting room, surgery, maternity ward. The consulting rooms each contained a narrow couch made of wooden poles and held together with strips of bark. There was a laboratory, distinguished from the other rooms by an ageing microscope on the table in front of the unglazed window. The reason for the hour's delay now became clear: the surgeon needed to put on his gown, his colleagues needed to get out for the journalist's inspection the microscope and scalpels which the dwindling army had been carrying from place to place, relics of a time when western countries considered UNITA a worthy recipient of donor aid.

I asked the camp commandant how long it had taken to organise what was happening at Calala. He replied in statistics as neat as the roads that cut through the forest.

'In effect, it was founded on 20 April – it has been in existence 49 days. We have gathered 4 700 people. People are still arriving, but in reduced numbers now. About 1 134 of them are soldiers – the others are family members, including men, women and children.'

Would UNITA fight again?

'No Angolan wants war any more,' the commandant pronoun-ced. 'If anyone thinks there is a will to go back to war, this does not exist.'

I suggested that no Angolans wanted war in 1992 either; the commandant insisted that things now were not as they were back then, though he was short on the specifics and invoked the mystic power of *situação*:

'In 1992 there was that situation, and Lusaka [the 1994 peace accord] was that situation and the combat continued. But since 4 April and the signing of the Memorandum of Understanding, the situation has changed completely – everyone wants peace.'

Of course, I wanted him to say that it was Savimbi's death that had made everything different. But he would not.

'There are voices who say this but I cannot confirm this since I am a soldier – following orders.'

The 'following orders' mentality extended to the commandant's grasp of the future as well.

'How much time will you need for demobilisation?' I asked.

'That is in the calendar set out in the Memorandum of Understanding. We in the quartering areas we will follow what is prescribed.

'Do you think your soldiers will want to go home after that?'

'According to the programme of the Memorandum of Understanding, people will receive technical or professional education. But there will always be people who want to go home, and they can do as they wish.'

'But do you detect goodwill on the part of the government?'

'It is set down in the Memorandum, at a high level. So we have confidence in this.'

In one aspect, though, the Luena agreement had been disregarded completely. In setting out the plans for the quartering areas, the memorandum had prescribed adjacent but separate camps for soldiers and for civilians. This had been written in as a political nicety: there were still lingering memories of 1993, when UNITA allowed food aid into besieged towns on condition that half of it went to UNITA – often to sustain the guerrillas themselves. The authors of the Luena agreement had tried to separate civilians and soldiers so as to let foreign donors send food aid to women and children without the embarrassment of being seen to feed the military.

Yet at Calala soldiers and families lived in the same houses. When I asked the commandant why, he seemed to have overlooked that clause in the agreement.

'UNITA's soldiers always lived with their families. That was UNITA's way.'

Later I would discover that within UNITA the distinction between a soldier and a civilian was fuzzy in any case.

At the 'technical area' near the entrance gate – the place where the FAA officers were stationed to oversee demobilisation – children stared silently at the weapons, mostly AK-47 assault rifles, laid out on tables under the trees. I found the soldier on duty asleep across two aircraft seats in a small *jango*; he awoke apologetically and went to fetch his commanding officer. When I asked the colonel how the seats had come to be there, he said it was the '*situação da guerra*' – the situation of war.

The FAA colonel declared that his task of disarming UNITA's men was almost complete, although the weapons that had been handed in numbered no more than 100. If there were really more than a thousand soldiers in the camp, this low tally of surrendered weapons was worrying.

None of the people I talked to as I wandered through the forest paths of Calala, all speaking the same eloquent but rather formal Portuguese, would admit that Savimbi ever did anything wrong.

'I was with UNITA a long time, at least 20 years,' recalled one venerable.

'It was a just cause so I decided to fight with them. We can never forget the ideas of our president.'

'What ideals?'

'Patriotism.'

He had been in Luanda at election time, before going back to the bush once more.

'We went back to the *mata* to fight for our cause, a just cause.'

'Do you think Dos Santos won the 1992 elections?'

'I can't talk about that – it's a bit sensitive for me.'

Adriano Keto had also been in Luanda in 1992. His father was the chief of police in Sambizanga, in the *bairros* of the capital. Adriano himself had been born in Sambizanga and had originally gone to Savimbi's bush capital, Jamba, in 1980. In that year he would have been only 12 years old. His story of taking up arms five years later was one that I would hear in numerous subsequent conversations with men who had spent all or part of their childhood in UNITA's ranks.

The life stories had a curiously mathematical precision; it was rare for anyone to admit to having entered combat before the age of 16. Nor would Adriano say what had prompted the move from Luanda to Jamba, a 1 500-kilometre diagonal journey across Angola.

'I saw my family in September 1992 and we separated then; since then I never saw them again. I have been in the *mata* all this time – now that peace has come I will soon be privileged enough to meet my family without problems.'

For 'peace has come' he said *'paz surgiu'* (peace has risen up), as though he were talking about a supernatural, apocalyptic event rather than a political process. *Paz* could appear as arbitrarily as any other *situação*, and it was nobody's business to ask where it came from or how long it would stay around.

He took a page of my notebook so he could write a letter, and asked me to try to find his father in Sambizanga.

Before we left Calala we sat down to eat. It was difficult to accept a meal from people who believed themselves to be at risk from malnutrition but the commandant insisted, in a formal address before the meal: 'It is an African tradition that we cannot let our guests go hungry.'

The rough table was crammed with plates of rice, fuba and stringy *carne de caça* from some buck that had been killed or trapped in the bush. The commandant apologised that we would have to eat with our plates on our laps: *'não temos condições de mesa'* (we do not have the conditions of a table) – the ability of the Portuguese language in the mouths of Angolans to turn a lack of furniture into an issue of social development.

This show of self-sufficiency was at odds with the picture the camp commandant painted: 'The quantities of food that are coming in are not enough to sustain the number of people we have here. We received food from the FAA but only enough to sustain us for two, three, maximum four days. We are obliged to go to the bush and gather honey – it is the only resource we have here.'

Whatever the privations, the inhabitants of Calala seemed to be bearing up remarkably well. The MSF team went ahead with their task of vaccinating children against measles, but said the children seemed better nourished than the medics had expected.

As we drove away, the driver went the wrong way around the roundabout. The Angolan MSF staff riding on the bakkie shrieked with laughter. *'Violou!'* (He broke the law!) Ahead of us, the sun set, an opaque pink disc that had surrendered its luminosity to the dust that surrounded it. The headlights ploughed through the gold-coloured grass that overhung the road back to Cazombo.

❖

Cazombo sprawls along both sides of the single street that runs from the airstrip, past an echoing school and hospital building, to the oldest part of town where tile-roofed colonial villas are screened by the tortured shapes and thick scent of frangipani trees. Beyond lay a small open field of dry grass with a water tower and a vast satellite dish. Across the road from the satellite dish was the *palácio*, where the administrator spent much of his time in front of the television noting down the scores coming in from the football World Cup in Japan and Korea.

As in Cuemba, it was at the administrator's house that we stayed. But this *palácio* was better appointed than the one in Cuemba, newly plastered and painted, with glass in the windows. A squat man with a built-in sneer on his lips, the administrator had the only electricity in town, which fed his television, his lights and a single street lamp outside his house. The private diesel generator was situated sufficiently far away for someone else to be troubled by its noise. During meals, a servant would stand silently beside the table, while the administrator yelled 'Bread!' or 'Coffee!'

The administrator was a native of this area, of this geometrical protuberance of Angola so far from the Atlantic that Cazombo is only a short distance from the upper reaches of the Zambezi River. The sudsy water from the stream below the town that served as a public bath made its way east, over the Victoria Falls and eventually to the Indian Ocean. The administrator had joined the MPLA in Cazombo, before serving his time in Luanda. He bore no mandate from the people of Cazombo; Angola's administrators are all appointed from Luanda, just as the colonial officials of old were appointed from Lisbon. This post, this outpost, was his reward: a post where it was in his power to make the solitary street light shine, where nothing and no one could restrain him from humiliating an illiterate serving maid when she passed the sugar instead of the salt.

Beyond the *palácio* were the barn-like shells that had been shops or warehouses before independence, and where Angola's more recent history was now painted on the walls. One bore UNITA slogans from the last occupation, which had ended only in 2000. Across the road, a roofless, burnt-out concrete box filled with rubble and garbage carried the blue-painted logo of the UN High Commissioner for Refugees, a relic of the optimism that had come with the peace of 1991, when the UN came to ease the return of refugees from Zambia.

The UN had not yet returned, but the refugees had started arriving a month ago. Every afternoon, two or three army trucks would materialise out of a distant dust-cloud, and growl to a halt outside another of the warehouses, where the cargo of people would jump down. Behind the line of buildings on the single street, paths led to mud-brick houses, and beyond that to a field where the refugees had started building shelters.

In one of the huts – it had four walls and a door, but as yet no roof – lived Beston and Tobias. Both were in their twenties, both recently arrived from Zambia. They spoke no Portuguese; only the local Luvala language and the idiosyncratic English in which Beston described his situation:

'We are happy, we are enjoying so far. We are in our country, we have got to enjoy and utilise our resources in this place – we don't regret anything – we are happy about it and are here to do what we can because we have done a lot of things also in Zambia and as repatriates in this country we are going to do something better in this place.'

He and Tobias were living in one of the grass huts, 'waiting for well-wishers from other places to come and help us and then see how we can live in our place.'

Beston showed me two books: a Bible and an anti-Catholic paperback called *The Sunday Law*, published by the Seventh Day Adventists. The cover showed a map of the United States, with the Vatican flag skewered into Washington DC.

Tobias had left Angola for Zambia with his parents in 1983, when he was seven years old. The family had spent some time in Kabwe in the heart of Zambia, nearly 1 000 kilometres from the Angolan border. Tobias said his father had worked as a lecturer; the family had clearly been well-established.

'I was a security officer, I have been a driver and a mechanic. But looking at the job situation there is no job security, and we are mostly underpaid in Zambia. We thought that having a lot of resources in Angola we may do something big.'

Looking around the field of flimsy grass shelters it was hard to imagine that Angola held the kind of promise that Tobias spoke of. Hardly anyone in the refugee quarter spoke Portuguese, not even the youth in the bright yellow shirt and patterned tie who introduced himself as Pedro, but who was called Peter most of the time: 'Just a few words – *bom dia* – ha ha.' Tobias and Benson translated for me from Luvala to English as I tried to hear the stories of the rest of the people in the encampment: the ones who did not have the young men's English skills and confidence; the ones who had come from the Mahewa refugee camp across the border and now survived by gathering sticks, selling them to the townsfolk of Cazombo, and then buying sweet potatoes the size of my thumb.

'We came from Mahewa with nothing,' said an ancient woman, wrapped in a few faded print cloths. 'We have been here since March – the government provided only two kilograms of food for each person. From that day until now we received nothing from the government – we are surviving like this, we have no hoes to cultivate.

'I went to Zambia in 1999. We left Mahewa to come here because there was no food. We thought, let's go back to our country which could be better.'

The dream of post-war prosperity over the border was what had drawn most people back to Angola. Crispé Gasepi had been in Zambia since 1983. He had returned to Angola with his pregant wife and a child, 'because Angola is our motherland where we get wealth, where we could survive, we thought maybe things could be better.'

Now he spent most of the day sitting alone in the dust.

'When we arrived here, we were hungry, we thought it was better to go and look for food. While we were trying to cross the river, they fell into the water and now they are dead – my wife and child.'

As we walked through the *bairro* between the refugee camp and the town, we passed a group of people sitting in the sun outside a house.

A woman smiled and greeted me. It took a moment to recognise her; the cringing servant from the administrator's house had, here among her own, turned into someone who was able to acknowledge me as a fellow human and not just as yet another guest of the master.

Not long after the visit to Cazombo, I had the chance to return to Kuito. In that same place where Geraldo Jalo, the truck driver, had told his stories of ambushes and mines, there was now plenty of evidence that you could drive to the city without risking being shot or burnt alive. The market seemed to have doubled in size. Surly young guys who had ridden trucks up from Luanda or Namibia sold big, tinny boom-box hi-fi sets, or presided over stalls of perfumes, body lotions and hair straightener. The women in the food section now stood behind pyramids of tinned sausages and sticky sweet condensed milk. This modest but new-found prosperity had leaked across the town too: a thatched building with a generator and a TV where you could watch umpteenth-hand videos; beauty salons in booths made of plastic sheeting with a hand-painted sign of an aspiring beauty queen, all nails, lips and sculpted hair; three bakeries when there was previously only one.

People were repairing their homes, using pale orange bricks and mortar to fill the spaces left by blasted concrete panels. The bricks arrived on ancient trucks, little more than a chassis, an engine and a rudimentary cab; plenty of these trucks were coming into town as we headed out, towards the quartering area of Ndele. I asked one of the aid agency drivers where the bricks came from.

'From the farms,' he said. 'People are collecting the bricks from abandoned colonial farmhouses and selling them in Kuito.'

Getting from Kuito to the quartering area involved crossing several rivers, marked by the usual broken skeleton of a bridge. Here the temporary bridges were solidly constructed out of logs. It was the UNITA troops from Ndele who had done the work; they knew that no food was going to get to their quartering area unless the bridges got fixed. So the commanding officer ordered teams of men to fix the bridges. Sometimes, UNITA could make things very simple.

When we arrived at Ndele – another settlement in a forest, with a hand-painted sign that said 'Welcome to Our Quartering Area' – the colonel in charge explained there was a lot more that his men could be doing to improve the roads, if only they were given the right tools and materials. '*Temos as condições humanas*,' he insisted (literally 'we have the human conditions', but with none of the implications of 'the human condition' in English – more like 'the human capacity' or, more prosaically, 'manpower').

Certainly, there did not seem to be very many pressing tasks to be done in the quartering area. Now that the first phase of building was over, people were starting to decorate. Ornate window frames were appearing, plaited out of grass. One man had woven strips of bark into the thatched wall of his hut to form the letters 'ANGOLA'.

At the 'technical area' – where they stored the weapons that had been surrendered – AKs and RPG launchers dangled from the gloomy hut's thatched ceiling. Since this section of the camp was run by the FAA, there was the usual *confusão* over who had *autorização* to speak to the press. Eventually the leader of the technical group, FAA Colonel Espadinho Afonso, stepped forward with a calculator.

'We have ...' He pressed some buttons. 'At this precise moment we are in charge of about 548 weapons.'

He reeled off the contents of the collection as though he were a museum guide: 'We have various types of arms: PKM, AKM, AKs, G3, Mauser, RPG-7, M-79, we have missiles, GP-25, a few pistols and some explosives.'

The FAA colonel said there were 2 100 soldiers at Ndele, and more who had yet to be registered. This meant that just over a quarter of the UNITA soldiers at Ndele had handed in guns.

The UNITA colonel brushed aside my concerns: 'The number of arms missing is because some of them may have got left behind in the bush. We are confident that the number of weapons handed in is right, because this quartering area did not take in only armed soldiers. There were also members of the party and civic structures, all of them are quartered here. And during the fighting, many arms were captured by the FAA.'

It was becoming more and more difficult to figure out who had been a soldier and who had been a civilian within UNITA. Unlike in Calala, the people of Ndele had constructed separate areas for soldiers and civilians, as defined in the Memorandum of Understanding, and the colonel proudly showed us the symmetrically designed camp. Yet the soldiers' quarters were empty.

'Owing to a lack of household utensils, the soldiers live with their families,' the colonel explained.

And was the demobilisation process going ahead on schedule?

'I am certain of this for we have received orientations from Kuito and Luanda.'

That faith in bureaucracy was what gave him certainty. The colonel was confident that there would never be a war again. Why then was there a war in the past, I asked him.

'It was our politicians who must explain the reasons for war in Angola – but ultimately we were fighting between brothers.'

It was an argument that I had heard before, and would hear many times again in the months that followed. Back in the town of Kuito, only one person dared question the orthodoxy that national reconciliation was as easy as signing a peace accord. I shall call him Simão; that is not his real name, but he did not want to be quoted on this particular concern.

Few could speak with greater authority than Simão, who now had a job with an aid agency and wore the comfortable fat of the African father who had won the means to be worthy of his role of patriarch. He had survived the siege of Kuito, when UNITA and the MPLA faced each other down from opposite sides of the main street, and when desperate groups of civilians would shoot their way through UNITA lines and spend weeks foraging in the countryside for food for the starving town.

'What will happen when the UNITA soldiers come and live in the *bairro*, and they could be living next to someone who lost a child or a mother or a friend?' he reflected.

❖

When I got back to Luanda, I set about trying to trace João Keto, the policeman father of Adriano from the Calala quartering area. I sent an e-mail to Francisco Pestana, the police press officer, who phoned back a few days later saying that João Keto was with him at the headquarters in the Cidade Baixa, a short drive from my flat. I went downstairs to meet them. On the pavement alongside the traffic that revved up the hill, next to the women selling baskets of bananas and pawpaws, I handed over the folded piece of paper to the wizened old man in his blue police overall.

At various times in his life, João Keto had believed four of his children to be dead. He had already managed to contact two of them. Now Adriano was the third to reappear.

'Do you think he looks like me?'

I couldn't honestly say I did, but pretended to.

'Is he thin?' Mr Keto must have heard the reports of people starving in the quartering areas.

'He is in good health,' I said.

João Keto had been through this too often before to be able to show any obvious signs of emotion.

6

The government wanted to recapture all the people

There was no time to count the graves in Chipindo. Some people said there were 2 000, others 4 000. Either figure was credible. The mounds of rusty earth stretched away into the bush, the dead lined up neatly and interspersed with the vegetation. This impromptu graveyard had appeared in the course of six months in the tiny town on the southern rim of the Planalto. Not all of the graves were marked, but some were topped with two strips of wood nailed together at right angles to form the simplest possible cross, with the names written in charcoal.

A rosary was wrapped around one grave marker. It apparently belonged to one 'Jervácio Dula Farseu Dias'. Then I realised that 'farseu' was *'falaceu'* (passed away); many Umbundu-speakers interchange L and R, and this was a phonetic transcription. 'Dias' was not the common Portuguese surname, but *'Dia 8'*, the eighth day of February 2002. Jervácio Dula had died on 8 February 2002. That was exactly two weeks before Jonas Savimbi died. Jervácio's death was not going to make history though. He was one of 2 000 or 3 000 or 4 000 dead in Chipindo, and who knew how many thousands in the whole of Angola. All the dates that were legible were between November 2001 and April 2002, the last six months of the war. Chipindo was currently home to 9 000 people. The graves suggested that at least a quarter of the local population had died in the space of six months.

I had flown to Lubango en route to Chipindo with a Reuters television team, and we had the end of the afternoon to enjoy the calm, the cool air and the ever-visible mountains that make even the briefest visit to that city seem like a holiday outside of Angola. Thanks to the television money that was behind this trip, we got to stay in Lubango's tourist resort up on the hill, a complex of tidy thatched bungalows with a good wine cellar in the restaurant and tame antelope wandering around the lawns. The next morning we headed east in a WFP Landcruiser. The road deteriorated into the usual series of potholes not far beyond the city. At Matala we drove across the river on the dam wall, part of the hydroelectric scheme that keeps Lubango supplied with electricity most of the time. The town's main street boasted a monument to Cuban-Angolan solidarity, crafted from bent metal like a garden gate.

Beyond Matala, the road cut straight through the bush. The surface was largely intact for want of traffic, but all the bridges along it had been blasted into V-shapes of concrete that rested in the water. Then the car had to scramble down the river bank to the low, temporary bridge of logs that was there to last the dry season. At one of the bridges, children played on wooden scooters; it was hard to know where they came from, since there were few signs of habitation along the road. Half a dozen wiry old men passed us at one point, marching briskly along the roadside with Kalashnikovs at their shoulder. 'They're UNITA,' said the WFP driver.

A little further on was an incongruous market: women sitting on their haunches, each in front of a basket of produce. The baskets contained only dry beans. In the woods behind the market, houses came into view, houses built under the trees as they had been at Calala. UNITA had been doing this for years, as a way of making its settlements invisible to enemy aircraft. Today, such a village was officially not meant to exist as all UNITA's people were supposed to be in the quartering areas.

But what did 'UNITA's people' mean anyway? The quartering areas had been set up to gather together the people who had been following UNITA marching columns. This scheme took no account of women such as these who were selling their beans by the roadside. They had not been on the run with UNITA, though they had almost certainly supplied the rebels with food, voluntarily or not. This place had somehow escaped the attention of the FAA during the war and had ducked the defence ministry's strategy of clearing UNITA's people off the land.

What happened when the government's strategy did go according to plan became clear in the course of a conversation later that night after we arrived at the MSF camp in Chipindo. I found Adelino and Bento hunched against the highland winter cold, next to a crackling fire at the gate of the camp where they worked as security guards. It was hard to see either of their faces, but the firelight revealed Adelino's silver hair, and his voice, too, spoke of a man older than his 43 years.

'All these people were UNITA people. In the past, the people were working in their fields and producing well. During this war the government forced all the people to come here, to government-held territory. All the food that the people had grown before the war remained behind, their animals too. There was death here. Every day, more than 20 or 30 people died.'

I asked him why he thought there had been a war in Angola.

'It happened like this – people were divided between UNITA and the government. But we all were Angolans. When this war broke out, the government wanted to recapture all the people – it didn't mean there were two different peoples.'

If it was Adelino who, with these words, provided the pithiest take on the Angolan war that I had yet heard, it was Bento, sitting by his side, who appeared one of its most tragic victims. Now in his early thirties, the course of his adult life had been determined by being in the wrong place at the wrong time. His Portuguese was limited, and he spoke as though the delivery of each word were an act of pain.

'My mother disappeared in the war. My father disappeared in the war. Grandfather, brother. I am alone here in Chipindo. I have no mother, no father, no brother, no sister.'

I asked him which side he had been on the war.

'During the war I was with the government.'

He must have been referring to the pre-1990 phase of the war, for he continued: 'After the separation of peace ... the separation ...' and his voice tailed off, as though he knew he had the wrong word but through repetition could somehow make it right. I tried to think of events that he might be referring to. 'Elections?' That was the prompt he needed.

'Elections, after the elections in '92, UNITA captured me. That was in '92. UNITA captured me.' Once again, he ran out of words in Portuguese, and started speaking Umbundu while Adelino translated.

'I went to the bush in '92 because after the elections UNITA reoccupied the area – after that, because of the government ...' his voice tailed off again. I tried another tack, asking him about where he came from.

He had been born in Malange, but during the peace that preceded the 1992 elections he had set off around the country to go into *candongo*; the informal trade that took shoes, soap, batteries, radios, from the ports to the country's most obscure villages. Other Angolans had previously told me of the confidence and optimism of that period as the roads opened up for the first time in living memory. Bento could not have known that his mercantile wanderings would lead him straight into the arms of UNITA just as the rebels were going back to war.

We had arrived in Chipindo minutes before nightfall, just long enough for the TV team to get some atmospheric shots of the blank orange sun setting behind the huts of the refugee settlement and the few standing walls that remained of the old village. It was then that the message came through: the plane that was to fly us out of Chipindo was leaving at seven the next morning. We had driven all day only to arrive at dusk and leave again at dawn.

The television people were confident that if the plane could be delayed by just a little, they would be able to squeeze in the shots they needed between sunrise and departure. So I went off in the dark to try and find people who could tell me what went on in Chipindo, and the firelight had led me to Adelino and Bento.

The Spanish aid workers from Acción Contra el Hambre let us spend the night on the floor of the large tent they used as an office at Chipindo. In my sleeping bag, and wearing every piece of clothing I had with me, I still woke several times from the cold. In the camp, people drummed and sang until late. I assumed it was a way of keeping warm since there was nothing to celebrate, except perhaps the knowledge of having defied the odds and stayed alive.

In the morning there was time to see the graves before the little plane arrived. But not to count them.

Corkscrew landings were still the order of the day for the UN flights. The war had been over for more than three months now, but security guidelines remained in place in case of a stray surface-to-air missile launcher that might be lurking in the bush in the Angolan hinterland. Besides, the pilots enjoyed the spiral plunges.

Usually, this meant that the destination town was already in sight when the descent began, and from 10 000 metres in the sky it was fun to make a quick guess about the place where we would be landing. Was it on a plain like Kuito, on a hill like Uige, or in a valley like Lubango? Did it have tree-lined avenues like Luena, or a big park like Huambo? As we started spiralling towards Mavinga, on the plains of Cuando Cubango province in Angola's far south-east, it seemed there was no town at all. It was the airfield, a straight strip torn out of the bush, that first caught the eye; only a few minutes later was it possible to make out, appended to the edge of the landing strip, the dozen or so buildings that made up Mavinga.

From the ground, the perspective was even less encouraging. For a start, it was an effort to walk the short distance from the airstrip to where the buildings began, since the street was as sandy as a beach. Few of the houses had roofs; many had holes in the walls or whole walls missing.

One such building was the hospital, distinguished by the skull and crossbones of a landmine warning sign dangling from its perimeter fence and *Viva o doutor Savimbi* painted on the exterior wall. There was no roof, just a tarpaulin tied to the rafters. This and other rudimentary repairs had been carried out by MSF. The only object obviously provided by the government was a poster of José

Eduardo dos Santos, tacked to the pitted wall inside the entrance. On the cement floor beneath it, a humped shape heaved under a grey blanket, each convulsion accompanied by a rasping choke. The noise was just about recognisable as one made by a human being in pain and distress, the shape less easy to resolve. A nurse explained later: what I took for catatonia was in fact a makeshift treatment for pneumonia. In the absence of other methods to drain the lungs, the patient crouches, backside in the air and mouth kissing the ground, to let gravity do its work. Other patients lay on their blankets on the floor, heads propped up against the shattered brickwork.

As the graffiti suggested, Mavinga had been the last municipal centre held by UNITA, and much of the visible damage had been done during the battle in 2000 when the FAA finally took the town from the rebels. Even after that, the thick woodland and the sheer size of the region had meant that UNITA retained the advantage in the countryside.

The Portuguese, whose colonial ventures seldom strayed this far from the sea, had nicknamed Cuando Cubango province *a terra ao fim do mundo* – the land at the end of the earth. Angola's present rulers, whose affinity for the coast was as strong as that of their European antecedents, seemed to take a similar view. After independence in 1975, and again after the 1992 elections, the MPLA had found itself in control of the seaboard and not much else, while UNITA sat squarely in its political heartland of the Planalto. On both occasions, the government's victory had been a matter of pushing UNITA out of the centre of the country, and driving the rebel army further east, into the interior. As was typical, the retreating UNITA troops took with them the people under their control. The inhospitable lands at the end of the earth now carried an incongruously large population.

After the war ended, the two UNITA quartering areas near Mavinga between them received 70 000 people – about a fifth of all the people in quartering areas in the entire country. For weeks, those quartering areas had received no food.

Those who survived the hunger had come to Mavinga for treatment. The MSF staff showed off a boy called Felizberto, one of the successes of their care. He had arrived starving; now he was still thin and barely spoke, but never stopped moving, devouring new people and objects with a stare that was many times stronger than his tiny body. He took hold of my minidisc recorder and pushed the buttons. I attempted a conversation with Felizberto's father, who sat heating water over a stick fire. He seemed to be deaf, but one statement that came through loud and clear was:

'I am a black Angolan – to defend my black skin, that is why I went with Savimbi.'

Also among the parents waiting in the sand of the hospital compound was a woman in a brightly coloured headscarf who had brought her child from the Matungo quartering area to be treated for malnutrition. She said there had been plenty of food in her village, but none when she arrived at Matungo. Why then, I asked, had she gone to the quartering area? Up until that point she had been talking in Umbundu, with one of the staff translating, but now she replied with a single Portuguese word: '*Paz.*' Peace.

Peace, as they said, was more than just a silencing of arms. For some, it was a word in a foreign language that meant UNITA commanders telling you to up sticks from your village and go and see your child starve in a quartering area.

Mavinga town itself had been all but abandoned when UNITA fled. The people who lived there now were the ones brought back by the FAA during its forays into the surrounding countryside. They lived in fields of grass huts on the edge of the town, which already occupied a bigger area than the perforated buildings that comprised the colonial town centre. I spoke to a woman in a lacy dress who was merely slim, in contrast to the emaciated figures at the feeding centre, and who had learnt to smile again. She said she had been in Mavinga since March, when she arrived from the *mata*. She laughed when I asked her why she had been in the *mata*.

'I was in the *mata* because of the war – always with UNITA, in the Capembe area. During the war we were always on the run, then we were caught by the government. So now we are here in Mavinga.'

'Are you still a member of UNITA?' I asked.

Again, she giggled as though I had asked a stupid question.

'No, now I'm a member of the government.'

'What makes you a member of the government?' I wondered.

'Because I am here with the government.'

So that was all it came down to. There were no UNITA people, there were no MPLA people. No UNITA supporters, no MPLA supporters. It was just a matter of who happened to be waving the gun over whichever acre of scrubland you happened to find yourself in at a particular moment.

The quartering areas were 40 kilometres from Mavinga, and I went there with a team from MSF that was carrying out an assessment visit. The driver of the Landcruiser described the road as *'muito péssima'*, a kind of double superlative and a most expressive abuse of Portuguese: 'very terrible'. In fact, there really was no road, just more or less visible tyre tracks in the heaped-up sand, and a more or less consistent passage through the bronze-coloured trees.

Three hours later, we emerged from the trees at the start of a grassy flood plain. Green-leafed vegetables sprouted from what Angolans call a *naka* – riverside land where the soil is damp enough for cultivation to go on through the dry season. Water lilies grew in the river where children had led long-horned cattle to drink; one boy stood and stared at the water, holding in his hand a single long lily stem. Men drove little two-wheeled donkey carts.

With its livestock and fields, Matungo did not look like a quartering area although, in UNITA style, the houses were set well back from the river so as to take advantage of the camouflage provided by the trees. The people did not look as though they had spent years on the run.

'Right up to 2001, these people were in their villages. They had fields, they had cattle, but they had to abandon their areas because of the war,' said Colonel Alberto Jango, the UNITA officer in charge of the area. He did not mention people like the woman at the feeding centre, who had been forced out of her village because of the peace. But the point remained the same: *a terra ao fim do mundo* was deep UNITA land, where the government had barely had a presence until right at the end.

Asked where their homes were, people named the provinces of the Planalto: Huambo, Bié, Huila. Their presence here in Cuando Cubango was the legacy of UNITA's two retreats to the south-east. One old man's response was particularly telling: 'I come from Silva Porto.' Silva Porto is what Kuito was called before 1975. The entire history of independent Angola seemed to have passed him by. He had been with UNITA. Angola, or rather the Angolan state that had its capital in Luanda, had been another country.

In the thatched shelter where I had spoken to the UNITA officers, Elias Chamissa, the teacher, had been giving English lessons. On the blackboard in the shelter proverbs were written:

'One swallow doesn't make a summer.'

'It takes two to make a quarrel.'

'A new broom sweeps clean.'

The northern climate implicit in the first proverb must have tested Mr Chamissa's pedagogical skills here in the tropical bushveld. The second held an obvious enough message for Angola, though perhaps not one that was easy to reconcile with the official UNITA syllabus. The third could doubtless have all sorts of implications for UNITA's ambition to govern. But for the moment, any notion of clean sweeping seemed a long way off.

It was 19 July. The government had announced 20 July as the deadline by which the token 5 000 UNITA soldiers were to be selected for incorporation into the FAA; the quartering areas were to be closed and the rest of the people sent back to their villages. But there was no sign of anyone packing up and leaving.

I asked the colonel what had happened to the plans.

'It hasn't begun yet,' he explained calmly. 'The date of 20 July is stipulated as the date for the process to start and we think that from tomorrow, the 20th, we will receive new orders to start the process of selection.'

Somewhere there had been a breakdown in communication. The lands at the end of the earth paid little heed to decisions made 1 500 kilometres away, on the Atlantic. When I asked Chamissa, the

English teacher, what would happen to Matungo after the soldiers left, he replied:

'That will depend on how many people stay here. When the soldiers have gone it will be up to these people to choose whether they want to remain here or go to where they have come from. There will be people of course who just remain here because that is where peace has started.'

Again, that was not what the government had had in mind when it signed the Luena accord. In fact, the last thing it wanted was for the rump of quartering areas to remain intact as villages whose loyalties would always be to UNITA.

The teacher's own plans were uncertain. He was from Huambo, but was unsure whether he still had relatives there: 'It's been a long time.'

As for the others, he said calmly: 'I think the international community will have to find some means to help these people learn new professions so they can start earning some money and live at peace.'

He made it sound so easy.

❖

We drove half an hour to Capembe, another quartering area in an almost identical riverside location. There too, there was no talk of demobilisation. In fact, they barely seemed in a hurry to gather UNITA's men from the surrounding area.

'In this area, not all of the troops are in the quartering area yet,' the UNITA brigadier said. 'In the peace accord it was agreed that the government would give help with transport to the troops who were far away.'

This last was either a misunderstanding or a deliberate lie. The Memorandum of Understanding had made no such provision.

The brigadier was reluctant to say how many soldiers had yet to arrive, but ventured: 'The last figure I have from a colleague who was in Rivungo was six thousand and something troops.'

Rivungo was about 200 kilometres further east, on the Zambian border.

❖

The MSF team's checks had identified one baby as needing urgent treatment at the makeshift hospital back in Mavinga. The mother and baby rode with us in the Landcruiser on that sandy non-road that made the journey a physical effort as tiring as walking as we leaned over or clung on to seats and window frames to counter the motion of the car. Night fell, leaving more than half an hour's journey to Mavinga. At a river crossing, the driver was unable to see the best way through the shallow stream and the car stuck fast in a reedy pit of mud at the edge of the road. Revving the engine produced noisy fountains of mud, digging got nowhere, and radio calls were unanswered.

Then lights appeared from the direction of Mavinga: a WFP car that made it across the river. Its driver used a winch to haul the MSF vehicle back onto solid ground. Our driver then backed the car away from the river, revved, dropped the clutch and charged forward into the water again. The momentum got him across. Through all this, the mother and the baby remained in the back of the car, making no complaint about the violent shaking they must have received.

The 'consulting room' at the hospital in Mavinga looked as if it had once been a kitchen, with whitish tiles on the cracked walls. The roof was completely absent from this wing of the building, and there was only a tarpaulin between us and the rapidly cooling winter night. The only piece of furniture in the 'consulting room' was a white plastic table, on which Dr Philip de Almeida laid out António, the baby from Matungo, who was now gasping and wheezing horribly. António's mother sat on the floor and watched.

Philip took the child's temperature and shook his head.

'He ought to have a fever – but he is so far gone he's not even producing the heat.'

With the flow of glucose in a drip tube inserted into the baby's arm, the body temperature began to rise and the doctor allowed himself a moment of elation: 'We did it!'

But his first impression had been correct. António had indeed been too far gone when he arrived. He died that night, the latest of about 200 children to die in Mavinga in two months.

Philip de Almeida was a Sri Lankan, now working at a hospital in Germany in between doing stints with MSF. 'I sometimes wonder what we are doing here,' he sighed one evening as he tried to grab a few hours' rest between the daytime routine and the nighttime emergencies. 'Two people are going to die tonight and there's nothing I can do about it.'

He talked about how the medical team at one of his previous postings, Sierra Leone, had had to prioritise whom to save and whom to let die.

'There was a woman who had trodden on a landmine and lost both legs. We gave her morphine. It would have taken me 40 minutes to perform a double amputation. But the man in charge said "No, what quality of life will she have?" '

After Sierra Leone, Liberia and Afghanistan, Philip despaired of Mavinga more bitterly than any other spot where he had been posted.

'I think, if there is a god, he is white and he forgot this place.'

❖

Back in Luanda, I tried to find out whether the government was serious about declaring the UNITA soldiers demobilised when not all of them had yet arrived in the quartering areas. I called an official in the presidential spokesman's office; he said that the fact that some soldiers, mostly in the east and south-east, had not reported for quartering created 'a complicated situation, an illegal situation'. The process was being postponed indefinitely, and 'technical teams' were to be sent to the quartering areas to assess the situation.

Situation or no situation, the formal demobilisation went ahead barely a week later. On 1 August 2002, the 5 000 UNITA soldiers whom the FAA had selected from volunteers in the quartering areas were officially drafted into the national army. The next day, 30 UNITA generals were allocated their new positions in the FAA, with UNITA's commander-in-chief, General Kamorteiro, taking the title of deputy chief of staff. The UNITA army that had once controlled most of Angola was signed out of existence. This meant that, abracadabra, there were no soldiers either in the quartering areas or wandering round the bush. There were merely 80 000 or so former soldiers in the quartering areas, and unknown numbers wandering round the bush.

❖

'*Boa noite, Mavinga!*' Good evening, Mavinga! The rock-star greeting drew not a whisper of response from the audience. They did not know how to behave at a rock concert since, not surprisingly for displaced people in Angola's most isolated province, they had never been to a rock concert before. Mavinga's population seemed as much shocked as fascinated by the coloured lights, the concert stage and the stacks of loudspeakers that had appeared on the sand of the main crossroads.

I asked a woman with a baby on her back what she thought of the music.

'I don't know,' she murmured. 'It's the music of the *Zairenses* (Congolese).'

It was December 2002, time for Angola's second solar eclipse in the space of 18 months. This eclipse was to pass over Angola from west to south-east, and the government had decided that, this time, Mavinga would be the official viewing spot for the event. The town was an unlikely tourist attraction. The food crisis had by now been brought under control, but the 100 000 people there and in the nearby quartering areas were surviving only by means of a massive airlift of food aid from foreign donors. The people at WFP were not happy about planes full of day-trippers tearing up a dirt airstrip that was barely adequate for the aircraft that brought in the food. Not only that but, five days before the eclipse, seven health workers based in Mavinga had been killed when a Landcruiser belonging to MSF had run over an anti-tank mine 70 kilometres from the town.

The viewing plans went ahead anyway. The government had invited a dozen or so foreign scientists to observe and photograph the eclipse. Their flights and accommodation – they were put up in five-star hotels for several days in Luanda, before going to Mavinga – were paid for by the education ministry. Government spending on education had frequently come in for criticism the previous year;

education had accounted for only five percent of state spending, with a large part of that going to bursaries for students at foreign universities. Teachers had become accustomed to going without salaries.

To ferry guests, including MPLA and opposition party officials, from Luanda to Mavinga, the government had chartered a Boeing 737 from TAAG, the state airline. The Boeing would take us to Menongue from where we would transfer to planes that could cope with the earth runway at Mavinga. On the tarmac at Luanda, a policeman gave our bags a cursory inspection. The man in front of me had a large pistol with him, and was told to check it in with his hold luggage. Why was he taking a pistol to Mavinga, I asked.

'To defend myself.'

A pistol seemed an unusual defence against landmines.

From Menongue, my flight was on an Antonov. People crammed onto the benches along each side or sat on the floor or on top of the crates of drinks while two sinuous young women in the Luanda uniform of tight pants and miniskirts passed round bottles of Castle Lager, opening them with their teeth. Disembarking at Mavinga, we made our way past the hospital compound with its 'Beware Mines' sign. The hospital now had a tin roof, courtesy of MSF; the government's own developmental efforts had been directed elsewhere. Further down the sandy road, the house that had been used by Acción Contra el Hambre as a base for distributing food – where a landmine had been found in the yard a few months ago – was barely recognisable. It was freshly plastered and painted pink, with tiles on the roof and glass in the windows. The humanitarian organisation had been thrown out and the premises renovated as a guesthouse for visiting dignitaries.

At the open-air stage that had been set up for the evening's concert a banner announced that the event had been organised by the National Spontaneous Movement. A cyber-café at the site was housed in a temporary building made of poles and tarpaulins, with a satellite connection to the internet. There was no opportunity to test whether it worked since the only computer was occupied by a young man playing an animated game that involved driving a police car through the streets of Chicago. A large thatched shelter served as a restaurant, with candles and flowers on the tables. Waiters used table knives to open the bottles – there was plenty of beer, but no one had thought to fly in a bottle opener.

Over dinner I chatted to some of the visiting scientists whom the government had flown in to view the event. They were not feeling completely at ease.

'It definitely feels awkward for European scientists coming with hi-tech gear to be in the middle of all this, but on the other hand maybe it brings something to the population here, and could be a way back to normal life,' said one.

Nearby was another temporary shelter where journalists, the junior opposition party delegates and other non-VIP guests bedded down for the night. The loudspeakers outside continued to pump out music to their bewildered audience.

Dawn was cloudy. The observers had set up their optical equipment in an open area between a bombed-out school and a refugee camp, and the light began to fade perceptibly soon after the sun rose. Through dark glasses it was possible to see the diminishing circle of the sun as long as the clouds were not in the way. For a time it looked as though the event would be a colossal flop – trying to view an eclipse during the rainy season was always going to be a risky undertaking – but the sun cleared the clouds seconds before the eclipse popped into totality, casting the sandy plain, the grass huts and the distant trees once again briefly into night.

After the sun had reappeared, I encountered the education minister, António Burity da Silva, strolling around in one of the zebra-striped Stetson-style hats which someone had had the good business sense to take to Mavinga and sell to the visitors. I asked the minister why on earth his ministry had decided to site this event in Mavinga.

'Firstly because according to scientific information it offered the best visibility, and secondly because we intend to transform this geographical region – which only a few months ago was the scene of violent conflict – into a place of harmony, development, democracy and progress,' he replied.

The following day we returned to the Mavinga airstrip which, according to an MSF staff member with a thick French accent, was now looking like 'Issereau' – he was referring to the airport in London. The two Hercules cargo planes chartered by WFP had been joined by the Antonovs and an assortment of light passenger aircraft, and it was on one of these that I found myself travelling back to Menongue along with the scientists. When we landed in the provincial capital, there was no plane to take us on to Luanda – instead, a lunch was scheduled at the governor's *palácio*, a long, low building that looked like a 1960s motel. Two bottles of Chivas Regal were passed around the table.

I found myself sitting next to a German scientist who was battling with the morality of government funds being used for a junket of the kind we had witnessed over the past 24 hours.

'But if this event hadn't happened, would the money have gone to the people?' he wondered. It was hard to imagine that it would have done.

We got into the four-by-fours for the trip back to the airport. A well-coifed *mestiça* lady from Luanda, also waiting for a plane, had the last word:

'So moving, two eclipses in a time of peace.'

7
Becoming normal

As the months went by after the signing of the April 2002 peace accord, UNITA's bosses seemed to be in no hurry to leave the Trópico Hotel. The payment of their bills there appeared to be the one, albeit unwritten, promise from the Luena talks that the government was determined to honour. The polo-shirted oil men continued to pass through on their way to the rigs in Cabinda, but they now shared the lobby with the men in dark suits and lapel pins with UNITA's black cockerel emblem, who had nowhere else to conduct the business of politics.

Much later, General Gato gave an interview to *Folha Oito* in which he was asked how he accounted for his transformation from the haggard guerrilla leader of February 2002 to the sleekly groomed politician that he had become by the end of that year.

'When I was at the Trópico, I was able to benefit from the gym,' he responded, adding that he had recently purchased an exercise machine to use at his new home in the affluent suburb of Vila Alice.

Discussing the vagaries of the talks between the government and UNITA with the journalist Gilberto Neto some time in the spring of 2002, I heard Gilberto use, quite unselfconsciously, the formulation 'Trópico says ...' when he meant the UNITA leadership, much as one might say 'the White House' or 'Downing Street' to refer to the American or British government. Among those who held court at the hotel was UNITA's foreign affairs official, Alcides Sakala, whose good English meant that he was the de facto UNITA spokesman, at least as far as the BBC was concerned. He was always effusively charming, and usually found time to talk. The biggest problem during radio interviews was trying to cut out the hotel lobby background noise: a recording of the *Titanic* theme played on panpipes, for example, or the cocktail-hour pianist playing tinkling arrangements of jazz standards.

One afternoon we sat out on the terrace by the deserted swimming pool, where the main irritation was the noise of the ornamental waterfall, and I asked him what he saw as UNITA's political priority.

'In Angola you have a minority class in this country, living well. Then if you go to Boavista you see that people are living in terrible conditions. There you don't find whites or *mestiços*, only blacks, and something has to be done for these people. It's a matter of justice. Angola is a very rich country from oil and diamonds. There is sufficient to supply these people with schools and hospitals.'

I could not help feeling that such talk with its left-wing implications of increased social investment and redistribution of wealth would have surprised UNITA's former sponsors, Ronald Reagan and PW Botha. After so many years of being associated with the right wing, was UNITA now positioning itself as the left?

Sakala chuckled and circumnavigated the question.

'That is a very complex issue. But we have to work for these people, the poor. If that means being on the left, OK. If that means being in the centre, OK. If that means being on the right, OK.'

UNITA had been Maoist when it drew support from China; Savimbi had been a convincing enough free-marketeer to get invited to Reagan's White House; Sakala was now talking about redistributing wealth to help the poor, but insisting this was nothing to do with ideology. By early 2003, the word 'socialism' would be appearing once again on UNITA's banners.

Sakala offered a similar explanation of how a professedly anti-racist organisation had ended up in an alliance with apartheid South Africa:

'It was a matter of circumstances and we had to survive that time within the framework of the Cold War. Why die here when there was the opportunity of fighting with others against communism? And we succeeded. UNITA was the only party fighting for democracy in this country in 1992. We broke from the past, from the one-party system.'

The Cold War alliances were as random as the ideologies. UNITA's political meanderings were no more incongruous than those of an MPLA that still attended meetings of the Socialist International while presiding over inequalities that rivalled anything created by apartheid. The fundamental difference between the two parties now was that the MPLA – or, more accurately put, a small group of people surrounding José Eduardo dos Santos – was in power and UNITA was not.

Was it this that explained the extraordinary charm of UNITA's leaders when dealing with journalists? During the coffee break at one UNITA public meeting in a Trópico conference hall, General Gato noticed me walk by, and interrupted the conversation he was having with a colleague to turn and shake my hand. For a journalist who had become used to dealing with days of un-returned phone-calls just to get a surly MPLA official to trot out the party line, such courtesy from a political leader was startling.

In the post-war lull that followed the signing of the Luena accord, it became too easy to forget that this was the same UNITA that had attacked Caxito, that had blown up the train in Zenza de Itombe. So it was useful to have the occasional reminder.

The first such reminder came as the result of an invitation by the International Committee of the Red Cross (ICRC) to accompany a team that was escorting two youths who were to be reunited with their families in Malange. António had been separated from his family during a UNITA attack; Miguel had been captured by UNITA and led around the country. Both had eventually been brought to an orphanage in Luanda. It was from there that we fetched them, before boarding the ICRC's plane at the airport.

António said he was 15 years old, though, like many Angolan adolescents, he had the searching eyes and the thin frame of a child several years younger. He had last seen his family three years before, when the war had separated him from his mother. He had been taken from Malange to Luanda in a vehicle, he said, but remembered nothing more. UNITA had frequently attacked Malange in 1999 and families had been scattered as people ran into the bush. It seemed likely that someone had found António, assumed he was lost or orphaned, and taken him along as they ran to Luanda.

Miguel was less talkative. He also said he was 15, but – in contrast to António and unusually for an Angolan – looked older. He said it was 'many years' since he had last seen his family, before UNITA captured him in the *bairro*. When I asked exactly how long ago it had been, he hesitated before offering 'three years'. With UNITA's eastward flight from the advancing FAA, Miguel had ended up in Moxico.

António's mother, Paulina, was waiting outside the ICRC office in Malange. She was as delicately built as her son, with a lined face and wide smile. She embraced António, letting go only to embrace the entire Red Cross team and me, in turn, before turning back to her son, who looked bewildered but happy.

'My son never said goodbye – there was all the *confusão* of the war, he never said goodbye.'

The second family reunion was more subdued. Miguel was met by his father, Domingos, a man whom Miguel so resembled that there could be no doubt as to their relationship. Domingos was beaming and proud, but Miguel showed no sign of recognising his father.

I asked Domingos when he when he had last seen his child.

'It's the first time since '92 – he's 20 years old now – I have the records and everything, he turned 20 on 3 May 2002. I never knew whether he was alive or not, until the Red Cross came to contact me.'

It was now clear why Miguel had appeared so big for his age – he was older than he himself realised. He would say nothing about his experiences in those 10 years with UNITA, which had taken him from boyhood through adolescence to adulthood. Whatever he may have undergone could only be guessed from his silence.

❖

The quartering area at Uamba provided a further reminder of what happened when children found themselves in UNITA's ranks. Situated in Uige province, near the border with the Democratic Republic of the Congo, Uamba was an abandoned colonial village, red bricks showing through the pink and yellow painted plaster of the old houses. The huts of the quartering area had been arranged outside the old settlement, but the dusty ground at the centre of the village still formed a focal point for the area. It was here that a group of puppyish youths in bandannas and baseball caps were gathered when our car pulled in.

'Were you soldiers?' I asked.

'Yes, we were soldiers.'

'Why did you join UNITA?'

'We were kidnapped.'

'How old were you when you were kidnapped by UNITA?'

'Twelve.'

'Do you think it's right to kidnap children?'

'Yes, it's right.'

Follow-up questions did not come easily.

The 150-kilometre journey from Uige to Uamba in a United Nations Landcruiser had been eventful. First there was the crossing at the Kuilo River, one of the many tributaries that carry water from this rainy area, down through forested valleys, to feed the fat Congo river. The steel girder bridge lay crumpled in the water, people with bundles on their heads walking tightrope along the remains. Even in the dry season, the Kuilo River is too wide and too deep for the kind of temporary wooden bridges that UNITA had been building in the Planalto. Instead, there was a raft: a few dozen oil drums with a platform of logs lashed on top. This was enough to float a minibus taxi, or its passengers, though not at the same time. The minibus would go first, and its passengers would follow with their sacks and crates. Peanuts and cassava were crossing the river from north to south. Dried fish and beer were moving from south to north.

The raft may have been a novelty, but it was nevertheless a fixed point in the journey. The road surface was less predictable. Unlike the rest of Angola it was not a question of potholes (which eat the tarmac from the inside) but of erosion gulleys on either side of the road that chewed at the margins of the tarmac until the road disappeared in a deep red scar. We came to a stop at one place like this, where there was a gaggle of soldiers and an army lorry by the roadside. At the bottom of the ravine, perhaps 30 metres down, an articulated army truck lay twisted on its side on the sand. Some soldiers were lashing cables to the fallen lorry, and these cables were attached to a second lorry that was wheezing and grunting as it tried to haul the dead weight out of the ravine. At the top, some of the soldiers were passing around a beer bottle.

Detaching himself from the group to answer my questions, the captain explained what had happened:

'You have to consider the speed; it was not possible to avoid an object that was in the way – doing 80 or 90 kilometres an hour one lost control, and this is how this situation occurred.'

The fatality of *situação* again, and it did not seem the situation would be reversed. When I asked the captain if accidents like this were a common occurrence, he did what so many minor figures of authority in Angola were wont to do and affected the attitude of one reading a prepared statement: 'In this province I can confirm that there have been many accidents of this kind. The roads here are in a critical condition – ravines are opening up, and though we can manage now, when the rainy season arrives it will be very difficult.'

Maria Flynn, the UN humanitarian coordinator for Uige, reckoned that four fifths of the province would be cut off from the outside world as soon as the rain started. Having lived through the bombardment of the city the previous year, she spoke with bewildered fascination about how, exactly one year later, she had found herself chatting socially in her living room with General Apolo, UNITA'S northern front commander who had ordered those same attacks. Apolo had given his word that UNITA troops would not interfere with the post-war humanitarian efforts. The problem was no longer ambushes but disappearing roads.

My original purpose in negotiating the road to Uamba had been to meet the Congolese rebel soldiers who, by virtue of opposing the Angolan government's allies in Kinshasa, had ended up fighting on the same side as UNITA. 'I'll take you to see the Banyamulenge', Maria had said, referring to the Tutsi fighters from eastern Congo who had supported Laurent Kabila in his quest for power, and then joined the rebellion against him.

The Congolese inhabited their own section on the edge of the camp at Uamba, a sullen place occupied only by soldiers, unlike the rest of the camp where most of the UNITA men were with their families. In the Congolese section there were no little boys playing ball, no women stamping manioc or girls carrying water, none of the things that frequently made the UNITA areas seem more like established villages than transit centres. Here, among the Congolese, there was nothing to disguise the fact that these men had, at the moment, no other purpose in life than to wait.

No one would admit to being Banyamulenge, but there were Congolese from every region of that huge country: from Kinshasa, from Kasai, from the Great Lakes region of the east.

'I am not Banyamulenge – I am pure *Congolais*,' said Moïse Akise. He had been in Kabila's Forces Armées Congolaises before finding himself among the soldiers who had turned against Kabila barely two years after bringing him to power. 'We have our party, the RCD, who are called rebels. I am here because of the situation in Congo – the bad job that our government is doing.'

The ubiquitous Portuguese *situação*, with its long, whining final vowel, was replaced here by the sibilant French *situation*, but the point was the same. Like the truck that fell over the cliff, the situation imposes itself without invitation, and mere human agency is powerless to change it.

Akise claimed to have been fighting only 'to protect ourselves' and not against the Angolan government. UNITA's people had at least the illusion of a common and noble purpose to sustain them. No so the Congolese, who realised that it was nothing but an absurd twist of history that had brought them to this forlorn place in a foreign country in which they had no interest.

The stories I listened to were as various and as incongruous as one could expect. Sergeant Papi Nezi dated his military career back to the days of Mobutu. He came from Kinshasa, and had started out in the Forces Armées Zaïroises at a time when Zaire was doing its best to destabilise Angola by backing UNITA. Yet living next door to Nezi was Captain Raphael Acolo from the central regions of the Congo who denied ever having been in any alliance with UNITA. His only common point of understanding with the Angolan rebels was a shared enmity for the Angolan army, which had entered Congo to prop up Kabila's precarious regime. All Acolo wanted now was to go home, and he believed he could do so with the intervention of international organisations.

'In the current situation there are openings, negotiations are beginning – we will go back.'

Just as it had been the situation that had landed them in this mess, so it would be another situation that would save them. Or so they hoped. As far as the international organisations were concerned, the Congolese had – like the truck – fallen down a crack. Since they were solders, the WFP was not allowed to supply them with food. The only international organisation that was mandated to help them was the ICRC, whose officials were under no illusions about what it would take to return 300 men to a country that was still divided between government and rebel control.

Two days later we drove the 300 kilometres from Uige to Luanda, setting off at dawn in the UN Landcruiser and soon plunging into a tunnel of rainforest. The journey seemed to be a descent all the way, whether gradual or steep. On the more exposed slopes the forest gave way to grassland, then a drop into a valley would engulf the car in more trees. All the way along, there were lorries that looked as though they had been patched, rather than serviced, for decades. Up until three months earlier, there would have been little reason for them to travel beyond city limits; now they had been commandeered to carry the weight of Angola's peacetime commerce.

Where the main road passed through the forest it was more like a country lane, with barely room for two cars to pass, and certainly no space for two trucks side by side. A broken-down lorry would occupy the entire width of the road. When this happened, the men would get off and use their machetes to hack a detour out of the forest. For all this improvisation, the triangular road-signs warning of a gentle curve or a series of wiggles were all meticulously in place. The Portuguese love of cement had reached even this far: the signs were all cast in concrete and, even if the years had left them chipped, they were still legible. The road had been so little used that there were few potholes. The greater obstacle to the driver was the cassava put out to dry by the local people who, in the years when this route saw only occasional traffic, had found another good use for a tarmac surface. Now the whitish tubers baked on the asphalt, turning grey with the grime of passing vehicles.

The road passed through towns, or rather through the remains of towns. One of these sat on the edge of the escarpment, where the road made a great sweep down towards the sea. It was called Vista Alegre, meaning 'happy view', the kind of candyfloss name that was given to any number of bland South African suburbs that sprang up in the 1950s or 1960s. That was a time when Afrikaners were moving from the farms to the cities, encouraged by the preferential treatment they received in the National Party-controlled civil service or in the burgeoning Afrikaner-run corporations. In Portugal, by contrast, the economy was not growing fast enough to absorb the motherland's growing population. So people went to the colonies instead.

When independence loomed and the settlers left, places like Vista Alegre fell into decay, the war preventing any urban settlement from taking root. People were living there again now, and were creating a new economy in the shell of a town that had been built for other purposes. It was hard to tell what had been a bakery, what had been a post office, what had been a bank. Each was now a shop, selling whatever could be found to whoever had the means to buy; each had its tins of sausages, tomato paste or beer arrayed meagrely along the windowsill. Another town seemed to have lost even its name. It bore a pockmarked metal signboard with the old winged horse logo advertising Mobil petrol. There was no longer petrol of any brand to be had there. Our driver radioed his base to report that we had now passed safely through 'Mobil'.

The road became worse and worse as we entered the area where cars had been daring to venture from Luanda, even during the war. By the time we were on level ground again, the road was more pothole than tarmac, and the leaves and thorns of the scrubland were coated in copper-coloured dust from the traffic.

Kofi Annan was coming to town. The UN, it was true, had been little more than an observer to the developments that followed the death of Jonas Savimbi while the Angolan government stage-managed the talks with UNITA. The beginning of August 2002 had seen UNITA's army signed out of existence, even though there were still 100 000 former soldiers in the quartering areas and no one from outside the FAA or UNITA had been able to monitor the surrender of weapons. The UN secretary general's visit to Angola later that month was to mark the UN's official re-entry into the peace process.

Legally speaking, the Angolan peace process was still governed by the Lusaka Protocol of 1994, which had been initiated under UN auspices in an attempt to pacify the country after the two years of fighting that had followed the elections. The Lusaka accord involved a ceasefire, alongside measures to put an end to a situation where two rival armies controlled parts of the country by force. UNITA generals were to receive positions within the FAA and an unspecified number of UNITA soldiers were to be incorporated into the national police. Territory controlled by the rebels was to be handed over to government control. In return, UNITA was to be allocated a certain number of government posts – in central and provincial government and in the diplomatic service – which would be filled with nominees of UNITA's own choosing. The UN was to verify the implementation of the Lusaka agreement. The international body was also to supervise the completion of the electoral process – the second round of presidential elections – and to take responsibility for matters pertaining to 'national reconciliation'.

The signing of the 1994 Lusaka accord had proved inauspicious: Savimbi declined to put his name to the document, sending instead his then secretary general, Eugénio Manuvakola. UNITA dragged its feet on relinquishing control of territory, and both sides violated the ceasefire; by 1998 it had become clear that the government, which had been distrustful of Lusaka from the start, intended to beat UNITA by force of arms.

Nevertheless, when the FAA and UNITA's generals sat down in Luena after Savimbi's death, they acknowledged that the Lusaka agreement still held legal force. The Memorandum of Understanding that came out of Luena was essentially a technical plan to allow the commitments made at Lusaka to become, belatedly, a reality. Implementation of the Lusaka Protocol was the responsibility of a body called the Joint Commission, chaired by the UN and comprising representatives of the government and UNITA. The Joint Commission had faded away after 1998 as renewed war made nonsense of the Lusaka agreement, but had now been convened once again.

For UNITA, the Commission appeared the best chance of winning concessions from a government which, ever since Savimbi's death had left the rebel leadership in disarray, had been dictating the terms on which the peace talks were conducted. UNITA's material rewards from Lusaka – positions in government – were clearly defined. But the Commission's mandate to look after 'national reconciliation' appeared to offer UNITA room for negotiation. It could put pressure on the government to loosen its grip on the state media, and to be more rigorous about separating the functions of the state from those of the ruling party. It could also, perhaps, allow UNITA the space in which to advocate the needs of its former soldiers, those who were still biding their time in the quartering areas. The Joint Commission was UNITA's last chance in the limelight before it sank back into the workaday functions of a parliamentary opposition party, and everyone was expecting the former rebels to take the chance to milk every possible concession.

Those Angolans who were sick of seeing the country's future defined by two rival armies were also hoping to see some benefit from the UN's return to the peace talks. The priests, lawyers, intellectuals and civic leaders who made up the civilian peace movement held a public meeting in September to discuss a 'complementary peace and reconciliation agenda' that set out its own interpretation of the principles of peace and reconciliation that the Lusaka Protocol had alluded to. A document circulated at the meeting set out a vision of the future that went beyond the demobilisation plans agreed at Luena: 'Peace is not merely the absence of the armed conflict, but rather the existence of political, economic and social conditions that might allow all Angolans to live in a harmonious way, evolving with justice and exercising rights of citizenship that might consolidate the democratic state and the rule of law …

'National reconciliation … should be based on the following principles: tolerance and acceptance of differences of any kind; respect for the rule of law, for human rights and fundamental freedoms; condemnation of violence as a means of conflict resolution and the use of the media as a means of pacification and of consolidating the democratic process.'

As Kofi Annan's visit drew closer there was some curiosity over what exactly his programme would be – whose vision of Angola's future he would be endorsing. We knew the secretary general was to witness the signing of an agreement by the government and UNITA committing themselves to implementing the outstanding matters of the Lusaka accord, marking, in effect, the transition from the military to the political phase of the peace process. Further than that, even officials at the UN compound seemed to be in the dark about Annan's agenda. The government, with either the cooperation or the compliance of UNITA, seemed to be determining the course of events.

A few weeks earlier, the UN Security Council had approved a renewed mandate for the UN's political mission in Angola. However, the report Annan's office submitted to the Security Council setting out the terms for UN intervention appeared to be way out of date. Among the main tasks that it foresaw for the UN was 'to provide technical advice to and general observation of the quartering, demobilization and reintegration process, if so requested by the Government of Angola'. The government had not made such a request, nor was it likely to since it had, meanwhile, declared the quartering, demobilisation and reintegration process to be complete. The report recommended the deployment of 'military liaison officers' to facilitate contact between the FAA and UNITA – even though UNITA's army no longer existed and its generals had either retired or been given jobs in the FAA. The UN, it appeared, had found itself overtaken by events in Angola.

In the two days leading up to the secretary general's arrival, it proved impossible to get hold of a spokesman from either the government or UNITA. From the government, this was hardly a surprise, but on the UNITA side even the normally obliging Sakala kept postponing appointments. It became clear that UNITA's steering committee was engaged in talks with a government delegation, but as to what they were talking about, no one was quite sure.

On Friday evening – Annan was due to arrive on Monday morning – the news got out on Rádio Ecclésia. The government and UNITA had agreed to restrict the Joint Commission's mandate to a period of 45 days. A month and a half to transform a war-ravaged autocracy into a working democracy. Even the diplomats of the troika, Portugal, Russia and the US – their noses out of joint that the government and UNITA had been talking behind their backs – were startled by the decision. There could be little doubt that the government wanted the Joint Commission to do little more than to supervise straightforward bureaucratic tasks such as UNITA's selection of incumbents for the government posts it had been offered at Lusaka.

The Trópico's cocktail lounge, as always, proved to be the best place to buttonhole UNITA. As Sakala made his way from a conference hall to a car, I asked him why on earth UNITA had agreed to the 45-day limit on the mediation process.

'It was a compromise,' he said. 'The government wanted 20 days.'

Weeks later, one of the UN's officials in Luanda told how Kofi Annan had been presented on arrival with a plan, endorsed by

UNITA as well as by the government, which set narrow limits on the functions that the UN was to fulfil. Annan, the official said, had been furious, and had considered staying away from the inaugural meeting of the Joint Commission. It went ahead, however, in the strangely frivolous setting of the Tropical ballroom, a glitzy reception venue more accustomed to high society weddings than to affairs of state. A pale blue banner decorated with fluffy white doves decorated the stage. Government ministers emerged from their individual limousines; members of the UNITA delegation unwound themselves from a battered Toyota, trying to get the creases out of their suits.

The event was chaired by Roberto de Almeida, the speaker of parliament. In his welcoming comments he referred to the government delegation as 'the Angolan delegation'. He subsequently apologised for the implication that UNITA's delegates were not Angolan, but it had been a telling Freudian slip.

Ever the diplomat, Annan addressed the gathering: 'It is significant that the ceasefire that was signed in April was done by Angolans themselves without third party participation, and it has held,' he declared. It was an exceptionally restrained remark, coming as it did from the head of a third party that had just had the door slammed in its face.

Annan had visited Angola on his way to the World Summit on Sustainable Development in Johannesburg. Colin Powell, the American secretary of state, was at the same summit and paid a visit to Luanda on his way back. The new roundabout and flyover at the airport, the construction of which had provoked monumental traffic jams and kept residents of the nearby flats without running water for six months, had been completed just a bit too late to be inaugurated on President dos Santos's birthday in August. It was ready, however, in time for Powell to make a quick exit from the airport. Just as well, since he was staying for only a few hours.

The American embassy had instructed journalists that if we wanted to see or hear the secretary of state, we had to be there to meet him at the airport and board buses that would travel in convoy back into town. It was an educational experience, being for once inside a motorcade of the kind that regularly gridlocked the whole of central Luanda. Once we were past the brand new flyover system, we sped along an unusually carless Avenida Ho Chi Minh, a thoroughfare lined with trees, flowerbeds and schools, before traffic police waved us around an illegal left turn towards the Trópico Hotel where Powell was to address the Joint Commission. The secretary of state continued to the Presidential Palace for a brief meeting with Dos Santos while the rest of us had our bags, our pockets, our shoes searched at least twice. Eventually, Powell entered the conference room via the emergency exit and uttered his words of encouragement to the government and UNITA.

'If it is to succeed, the Joint Commission cannot just become a mechanical exercise without meaning to anyone other than the participants. The Joint Commission and the healing it is meant to foster must be an instrument to build a new Angola, a peaceful, democratic and prosperous Angola'.

Powell took no questions from the local media (only days earlier, he had been jeered during the Johannesburg summit). The entourage of journalists travelling with him received their briefing notes on Angola from US embassy staff. We left the Trópico and drove in the buses back to the airport to fetch our cars.

Powell's address to an audience of MPLA and UNITA officials had been a neat reminder of how flexible (to put it euphemistically) American policy towards Angola had been since the days of the independence struggle. Washington's first ventures into Angolan affairs had involved neither of the two parties that now sat in the Trópico, but instead the FNLA of Holden Roberto who, 30 years earlier, had looked set to be the first president of an independent Angola.

Roberto had emerged as a nationalist leader in the late 1950s, organising among Angolan Bakongo exiles in what was then the Belgian Congo to found the União das Populações do Norte de Angola (UPNA – People's Union of Northern Angola). He later dropped the 'Norte' in an attempt to garner credibility as a national liberation movement. Travelling around the continent, he made contact with Frantz Fanon and African liberation luminaries such as Kenneth Kaunda and Patrice Lumumba. In 1961 the UPA started to organise a guerrilla army and, by 1963, a merger with another nationalist group had led to the formation of the Frente Nacional para a Libertação de Angola (FNLA). By this time, the MPLA had emerged as the FNLA's rival for international attention. Roberto declared a government in exile, which for a time won the recognition of the Organisation of African Unity as the sole representative of the Angolan people. In 1966, the FNLA's claims to being a national movement took a blow when Jonas Savimbi and his Ovimbundu followers broke away to form UNITA. But, as independence approached and the United States panicked over the prospect of the MPLA leading Angola into the Soviet sphere of influence, it was still Holden Roberto who was the object of the CIA's attentions as his army extended its influence southwards towards Luanda.

Limited American backing did not save the FNLA army from being routed on the northern edge of Luanda after the MPLA took delivery of Redeye missiles from Cuba. Following the political debacle of the Vietnam War, the CIA's commitment to its proxies in Angola was half-hearted, and US plans did not include the rearming of the FNLA. (John Stockwell, who headed the CIA programme in Angola, has written in a disillusioned memoir titled *In Search of Enemies* that the American strategy was not so much to install a surrogate government in Angola as to engage the MPLA in a perpetual stalemate.) For the MPLA's other foreign adversary, South Africa, there was no point in backing a rebel movement whose operations were confined to the north. Instead, South Africa gave its support to UNITA.

Holden sought exile in the United States, returning in time for the 1992 elections, in which the FNLA gained three parliamentary seats. Now approaching 80, he retained the figurehead leadership of the FNLA, but when people addressed him as *Mais Velho* (The Elder), the title was sometimes tinged with irony. These days he had little to fill his time with apart from pronouncing on what was wrong with contemporary Angola.

'All Angolans are cowards – they don't stand up for themselves – that's what 500 years of colonialism have done,' I once heard him remark. 'But people from the north are different.'

That proviso was inevitable, given the origins of the people Roberto considered his own. I recalled the remark some months later, when I read Stockwell's opinion in his memoir that Roberto had never seen active service. *Mais Velho* continued: 'There are three things one should die for, in order: nation, family, religion.'

I was about to say that the only time I was called on to die for my country it was to invade Angola and defend an unjust system in South Africa. Then I realised that from Holden's perspective, however often he might drop the name of Frantz Fanon into his conversation, the army of white South Africa had been on the right side.

Colin Powell's exhortations to the Joint Commission that it work to build a more democratic Angola may well, therefore, have rung a little false, coming as they did from the representative of a state that had spent years doing its best to destabilise Angola and whose first choice of protégé was now a small sideshow in Angolan politics. There were no signs, however, that the Angolan government had paid any attention to the secretary of state's words.

'Normalisation' was starting to overtake 'reconciliation' as the political buzz-word of the day. The government seemed determined to press ahead with its plans to close the quartering areas on schedule, in October, until UNITA and the aid agencies pointed out that the demobilised soldiers and their families had nowhere else to go. It was as though the remnants of war were a mess unbecoming a country which was due to assume the presidency of the Southern African Development Community (SADC) in October, and a non-permanent seat on the UN Security Council in February.

The weeks leading up to the SADC summit in Luanda saw a frenzy of painting. Squadrons of street sweepers were deployed throughout the city centre after dark, and the crashed aircraft that had lain for years beside the airport runway were removed so as not to alarm the visiting presidents. This was in addition to the urban improvement projects: flyovers that never kept pace with the shiploads of second-hand Japanese cars being imported from Europe, and pretty public squares with lawns and fountains that were popping up all over the city centre. The *bairros* remained without running water, electricity or sewerage and children could sometimes be seen helping themselves to buckets of water from the sprinklers in the parks.

It was several weeks before Kofi Annan announced the appointment of Under-Secretary General Ibrahim Gambari as the Special Representative who would chair the Joint Commission. Meanwhile, the clock was ticking on the Commission's 45-day mandate. Gambari, a Nigerian career diplomat, had made several trips to Angola over the past year to brief the secretariat on developments. Returning, he installed himself in a suite on the top floor of the brand new Hotel Alvalade, a five-star 14-storey building with the best views in Luanda.

Gambari believed that the Commission's mandate could be lengthened if necessary, but was doubtful that the government would allow the mandate to be extended beyond two months. He was frank about how the government had managed to circumscribe the UN's role in the peace process, but promised that that the UN and the Joint Commission would consult as widely as possible within Angolan society on the shape of the final peace settlement. It seemed doubtful that there would be time.

In reality, the opinions of anyone other than the government and UNITA were ignored by the Joint Commission until November. By then, the UN was renting a large house, complete with sparkling swimming pool, as an office for Gambari and his staff. A dozen or so civic organisations and small political parties were invited along to put their views to the special representative. The hearings took place, however, at a time when the Commission had already made its decisions and was tying up the last legal niceties of its work.

By the end of that month, the Commission declared its task to be over. The UNITA leadership had expressed concern about the ongoing welfare of UNITA's supporters in the quartering areas; they were appeased with promises of 'continued discussions' with the government. 'National reconciliation' would be dealt with in the same way.

Angola was now officially normal. Peace had happened, and political reform could be left for another day.

❖

One area where the need for change seemed most pressing in Angola was in the way the government managed its money. Angolan corruption was legendary, and the evident lack of social spending compared with the country's huge oil revenues made it obvious enough that something was wrong. But for a journalist it was difficult to unearth the necessary hard data.

That changed with an investigation by the International Monetary Fund into the management of Angola's financial affairs. The report that the IMF compiled was confidential and for internal use only – the government had blocked its publication. However, copies leaked out and began circulating among the foreign non-governmental organisations in Luanda.

The report listed the sums of money that had disappeared from Angolan state finances each year from 1997 until 2001: a total of US $ 4.3 billion in five years. In 2001 alone, US $ 900 million were unaccounted for – a sum roughly five times the value of foreign donor assistance received by the country each year. It did not say where the missing money had gone, but in its overview of the political and economic situation in the country it spoke of 'extensive corruption' as one of the challenges faced by the government. According to the report:

'Frequent dialogue with the [Angolan] authorities and significant technical assistance in recent years has yielded little progress in the key areas of governance and fiscal transparency. There is virtually no public information on fiscal and external public borrowing, the state-owned oil company manages the country's oil-related receipts through an web of opaque offshore accounts, the central bank and other public companies suffer from poor internal controls and large operational deficits, and the weakness of basic economic data hampers the design and monitoring of a macroeconomic programme.

'Reported revenues from Sonangol [the state oil company] cannot easily be reconciled with its share of oil receipts ... Further complicating the monitoring of oil revenues from Sonangol, the company assumed some time ago complete control of foreign currency receipts from the oil sector, and stopped channelling them through the central bank as mandated by the law.'

Damning stuff indeed. Before writing anything about the report, I tried to find out what the government had to say. The finance ministry, aware that transparency was a good thing, now had a website and a spokesman, Bastos de Almeida. That, at least, was a pleasant change from most government departments where no one was ever authorised to say anything at all. I was able to meet De Almeida, an affable man who received me in his office which, in contrast to the ministry building's dingy corridors, was fitted out with air-conditioning, comfortable chairs, several telephones and family photographs. The private paper shredder next to his desk was particularly impressive.

'We have taken note of this via the media, and the government has publicly denied the existence of this sum of billions of dollars' discrepancy in the public accounts,' De Almeida told me. 'The government cannot confirm the existence of such a disparity.'

On a hot Saturday morning I walked around the streets of central Luanda asking people what they thought of the disappearance of four billion dollars. At the bakery, one teenage boy declared with delight: '*É corrupção*' (it's corruption), relishing every syllable. Many others were afraid to express an opinion. It was a man reading the Saturday papers on the terrace of one of the coffee shops, however, who delivered the most devastating assessment of the loss of the money.

'It's normal,' he said, barely bothering to look up from his newspaper.

8

The son of a snake is always a snake

The flares from the oil rigs made the overcast night sky glow orange, silhouetting the crucifixion statues on the seafront. At the Catholic Mission Church across the road, the meeting had begun some time before sunset, and finished well after dark. The Catholic youth of Cabinda had had a lot to say. Some of them nevertheless managed to be pithy.

'*O governo é o filho do colono – e o filho da cobra é sempre cobra.*' (The government is the son of the coloniser – and the son of a snake is always a snake.)

This received wild applause.

Another youth took a reasoned approach. 'As long as there is war there can be no solution – we want dialogue that will help us find paths to independence.'

He was met with a blaze of opposition.

'How can we have reconciliation between Angolans and us Cabindans when in our own neighbourhoods we cannot move around or speak freely? How can we have reconciliation between Angolans and Cabindans when the troops who are supposed to be protecting us are our prime enemies? How can we have negotiations when the government is attacking the interlocutor? We need not only an improvement in our living conditions, but independence for Cabinda. *Muito obrigado.*'

The rhetorical 'thank you' prompted applause that rose and roared back down from the lofty roof. There were easily a thousand people packed into the mission church under the gaze of the usual selection of mass-produced Portuguese plaster saints. A local mural artist had been at work as well, however, and bold African angels now worshipped an etiolated virgin in pastel blue.

Another speaker took the floor.

'In the past we were called Portuguese, because we had to be. Now we are called Angolans, again we're talking about something compulsory – but of our free will we are Cabindans. We are a country, not a province.'

Cabinda was still at war. The peace agreement signed in Luena held no sway there, since UNITA was not involved in the conflict. In the early 1960s, around the same time that the MPLA began its resistance to Portuguese rule, and a good five years before Savimbi had founded UNITA, a man named Luís Ranque Franque founded the *Frente para a Libertação do Enclave de Cabinda* (Front for the Liberation of the Cabinda Enclave), better known as FLEC. His aim was to fight for Cabinda's independence from Portugal, just as the MPLA was fighting for independence in Angola and FRELIMO in Mozambique. FLEC's case was based on the fact that Cabinda had originally fallen under the influence of the Portuguese not as part of the colony of Angola, but as a separate protectorate.

The snag was that Portugal had for decades been ignoring the distinction between the two territories. For administrative purposes, little Cabinda had been appended to the much larger Angola, which since the 1950s had been regarded as an overseas province of Portugal. After the 1974 coup, as the new government in Lisbon rushed through the independence of its colonies, it tried to engineer an agreement with the three Angolan independence movements. FNLA, MPLA and UNITA did not agree on much, but they did agree that Cabinda would remain the sovereign territory of an independent Angola.

After Angolan independence on 11 November 1975, FLEC carried on fighting, not against the Portuguese army but against the MPLA. Over time, the rebel movement had spawned at least two splinter groups: FLEC-Renovada and FLEC-FAC. Cabindans would refer to the rump of Ranque Franque's movement as FLEC-Original or FLEC *sem adjectivo* (without an adjective). The divisions worked to the government's advantage. FLEC was never much of a threat to Angola's security, especially since it did not have the means to attack the oil platforms off the Cabindan coast, which accounted for about half of Angolan oil revenues. As long as the war against UNITA continued, Angola had better things to do with its army.

That changed after Cruz Neto and Kamorteiro signed the peace accord on 4 April 2002. Suddenly, the FAA found itself with tens of thousands of troops, all trained up with no war to fight. So they went to Cabinda.

Travelling to Cabinda as a journalist was a very different experience from flying on the WFP planes. For a start, there was a coffee bar in the air-conditioned waiting lounge reserved for passengers on SAL, the light-aviation subsidiary of the state airline. I was with Landu Nkama, the chair of an environmental organisation that dealt, among other things, with oil spills in Cabinda. When we boarded the 12-seater plane, Landu was the only black passenger; the others were all expatriate oil employees.

It was October 2002. The sun had crossed the equator, and in Luanda the summer heat was starting to take hold. A luminous haze covered the ocean, and the city disappeared from view before we had even reached the edge of the urban mess. An hour later we dropped down and out of the mist, over a coast of baobabs and scrub. It was as though we had strayed no more than a few kilometres from Luanda. The plane lined up for its descent onto a runway with a few houses on either side – people strolling, in no hurry to get out of the way. This was Soyo, just south of the Congo River, and Angola's most important oil centre outside of Cabinda. Its airport building was a concrete shelter worthy of a suburban railway station, but there was an extension under construction, with brown aluminium window frames that spoke of plans for an air-conditioned lounge here too.

Up again, over the placid creeks of the Congo delta and the narrow strip of Congolese territory that separates Cabinda from the rest of Angola. Landu said there had been plans to build a bridge over the Congo River so as to cement, quite literally, Cabinda's links with Angola. The plan sounded like a *reductio ad absurdum* of the Luanda city government's urban development plans: when in doubt, build a bridge.

The immigration officials were there at Cabinda airport, checking passports. I presented them with a photocopy of mine; the passport itself was in Luanda with the Immigration Department, which was taking the customary two weeks to issue me with the exit visa I would need the next time I left the country. The official was not happy, and it was only with Landu's persuasion that I managed to get through at all. International arrivals formalities for internal flights were an absurdity anywhere in Angola, yet here – in a territory where the government was doing its best to assert its embattled sovereignty – the irony of a gratuitous frontier check was almost delicious enough to make up for the inconvenience.

An hour later I found myself sitting in a wooden shack in the centre of Cabinda, the province's synonymous main city, with Landu and his Cabindan colleague, Chicaia. The waiters inside the shack, one of many arranged around a dusty carpark, all wore waistcoats and bow-ties. A rat strolled out from behind the stainless steel espresso machine and wandered off underneath the linen-decked tables. Chicaia pointed to an identical eating-hut across the square: 'It was over there that FLEC captured the Portuguese.'

Kidnapping foreigners had been the only way that FLEC had managed to get noticed over the past few years. The Cabindan rebels had been in trouble since 1997, when Laurent Kabila and the band of assorted rebels he led from eastern Zaire gave the push to FLEC's old patron in Kinshasa, Mobutu Sese Seko. The Angolan government had hastened to support Kabila and, later, his son and successor, Joseph, in the country that had now been renamed the Democratic Republic of Congo. Having lived for over two decades with a neighbour that had supported both UNITA and FLEC, a friendly power on the long northern border was not an opportunity that Angola could let slip by.

The Cabindan rebels seemed then to realise that they had little hope of capturing any more territory than the pockets of rainforest that they already held, but that seizing the occasional expatriate worker would get Cabinda into the news in Europe or America. Even so, staging a kidnap in broad daylight in the centre of town was ambitious for a rebel movement that was supposedly holed up at the other end of the province.

'Does FLEC have people here?' I asked Chicaia.

'They're everywhere,' he replied.

FLEC was able to operate in the provincial capital using methods better known in bush warfare: its men were indistinguishable from the local population, the flats and *bairros* their bush. In May of the same year that the Portuguese had been 'captured' in the centre of town, a rocket-propelled grenade had landed suspiciously close to a vehicle that was transporting employees of ChevronTexaco. In Luanda at the time, I had phoned the petroleum company's national office to try and find out more and, although the public relations man denied that there was any threat, it appeared that the company had revised its security procedures. ChevronTexaco staff would henceforth be transported by helicopter from Cabinda airport to the ChevronTexaco compound at Malongo, about 20 kilometres from the town.

The FLEC as well as the FAA factor figured in plans for a trip the following day, intended to show the visitors – Landu, myself and the political commentator Justino Pinto de Andrade, who had also arrived from Luanda – something of life in rural northern Cabinda. As a *branco*, it seemed that I was something of a liability, whichever fighting force we might encounter. If there were a FAA roadblock, the presence of a *branco* would attract attention and could have us turned back. If we came within sight of FLEC, there probably would not be time to explain that the *branco* was not an expatriate oil employee. Soba Kongo, a traditional leader who was accompanying us, had said eventually that we were going to a village that had been under the control of FLEC but had recently been taken back by the FAA.

It was evident from the first drive that Cabinda's main city was no Kuito. The war here had been fought in the bush, and its scars were no more evident than in Luanda. The *bairros* and villages that clustered around the capital, with its neat peak of sixties concrete, seemed at the same time less wretched than Luanda's *musseques*. At every new building site there was a signboard labelling it as part of the social responsibility programme of one or another oil company. Every village that was in sight of the road had a communal water point: a brick structure with the date of its construction stamped in the plaster and stumps of pipes where the taps had been. Invariably the taps were missing.

At Malongo, the villages halted to make way for the ChevronTexaco compound, inside which were quarters for the expatriate staff who commuted between Houston and Cabinda, a month in each place. The face that the ChevronTexaco compound turned to the rest of Cabinda was a three-metre mesh fence along the road, topped with coils of razor wire. Boys selling packed lunches by the roadside gave us a small glimpse of the world within – each lunch pack was a plastic bag of plastic American goodies with names like 'Dinty Moore's Noodles and Chicken' and 'Eezy Snax Cheez 'n Crackers'. Routine issue from the oil company, they were sold by local staff to passing travellers for 150 kwanzas (about three dollars at the then prevailing rate).

All of Cabinda's oil wells, producing half a million barrels a day (56 percent of Angola's total oil output) were controlled by ChevronTexaco. By law, every oil concession in Angola was a 50-50 partnership between the Angolan state oil firm Sonangol and a consortium of multinational petroleum companies. Among the foreign consortium would be one 'operating partner', the majority shareholder who directed the workings of that concession. Oil, in turn, even before the petroleum price inflation that accompanied the 2003 Gulf War, contributed more than US$ 3 billion each year to the Angolan state's coffers. The foreigners put up the money and provided most of the technical expertise; Sonangol got its 50 percent of the profits plus the 'signature bonus', the undisclosed sum that the foreign partners had to pay when granted the concession. It was a hole in the accounting between Sonangol, the National Bank of Angola and the finance ministry that had allowed US$4.3 billion to disappear from view, as the International Monetary Fund had documented in its 2002 report.

Journalists who had been inside the ChevronTexaco compound in the days when visitors were still permitted described a slice of American suburbia clinging to the edge of Africa – a capsule inhabited by people who knew Cabinda only as an airport; the compound was as hermetically sealed as the West Berlin of the Cold War. But unlike Berlin, here in Cabinda the political alliances during the 1970s had been as capricious and as self-serving as anywhere else in Angola. At a time when the MPLA was preaching Marxism-Leninism, it had welcomed the presence of Gulf Oil (ChevronTexaco's predecessor) in Cabinda. Cuban troops had been deployed to guard the American oil installation, and the most serious attempted attack had come from a country that saw itself as firmly on the American side in the Cold War – South Africa.

That incident, in 1986, ended in the capture of Captain Wynand du Toit who had landed on the Cabindan coast by night with his men, carrying explosives to blow up a pipeline, an old AK-47 and some UNITA pamphlets that they intended to drop to make the attack look like the work of Savimbi's men. Du Toit spent more than a year in a Luanda jail before being returned to South Africa as part of a prisoner exchange.

Beyond the compound, the forest, which up until then had been patchy, merged into a mass of continuous vegetation: green darkness at midday on either side of the road. Anyone could have been watching the car from a few metres away without our knowing. It became obvious how FLEC had managed to keep going for as long as it had.

Some time later we turned off the main road onto a rutted track through the forest, emerging from the trees as the road led us up a hill to Necuto. Towards the top, the village came into view: colonial cottages, some of wood planks and others of crumbling plaster, looking down over a large clearing to where the forest began again. Smoke poured from the door of a cottage where two women were trying to get a fire going.

There were the inevitable lengthy welcomes at the parish priest's wooden house at the very top of the hill, but it took some persuading to get anyone to be interviewed. A man in his fifties, wearing a bold checked shirt, agreed to talk but would not let me make a note of his name. We chatted across the table in the gloom of the padre's living room, oil lamps on the table and a calendar picture of the Virgin Mary on the wall.

'When FLEC's forces and the government forces meet each other, the government soldiers turn against the people, take the people's things away – they have to flee from the shooting, into the bush. We greatly regret what the government says about Angola extending from Cabinda to the Cunene, that there is peace in 17 provinces of Angola when the government continues to send its forces to Cabinda.'

The difference between FLEC and the government troops, he said, was that FLEC lived with the people whereas the FAA would descend upon them, using the excuse of any action by FLEC to take people away and rob them of their possessions. He confirmed that the FAA presence had increased since Savimbi's death.

'When the government had stopped making *confusão* there, they sent more of them here.'

'How does FLEC support itself? Where does it get its weapons from?'

'The question of arms I can't explain. But they have fields, and some produce is sold – this is how they live. They move around a lot to areas where they can attack – but then they go back to where they are based.'

'So what's the solution to all this?' I asked.

'The government has to meet the politicians of Cabinda to solve this. Because we are tired of it. The government knows where they are. Dialogue is the only way to solve this, arms can solve nothing, this has already been going on for a long time – 1975 to now. They should call Cabindan politicians who are outside to sit down.'

'Can you remember what happened in 1975?'

'What happened was that the white Portuguese left without saying anything. FLEC was fighting, and the UPA from the sixties. Then the MPLA came – FLEC was obliged to retreat. But the MPLA had no support here. They came here by force of arms with the Cubans and Russians.'

On the opposite side of the house, cassava fields stretched down the hill to a large clearing. A substantial church was under construction, the bare cement-block walls already extending all the way up to the gables, wooden door frames and windows in place. Two men were mixing heaps of cement and slapping it into moulds to make more blocks. Nearby, an incomplete school building had a signboard indicating it was the work of the Social Support Fund, which channelled World Bank money into development. It was a reminder that Cabindans' complaints about economic deprivation were relative. They were poor, for certain, but no worse off than most other Angolans.

The scene suggested the germ of a functioning society, a long way from the battle-shattered shells that central Angola's towns had become. This area had been controlled by FLEC, and more recently by the government. There were no signs of a missile or even a bullet having been fired when it changed hands. This seemed to be a different kind of war. Had the villagers capitulated without a shot? The FAA did not appear to have done much, meanwhile, to win the hearts and minds of the population. People's reluctance to be interviewed suggested they knew they could not speak their minds, yet neither could they bring themselves to endorse the authority of the government.

On the way back, leaving the forest behind, we stopped where several hundred people were building palm-thatched shelters by the roadside. The car seemed horribly visible in this exposed location and I felt equally exposed as I walked towards the nearest group of people. There was shuffling and blank stares before the group resolved who was to speak to me first, and then a man called Joaquim, only in his thirties but with a patriarchal bearing, appointed himself spokesman.

I started with the obvious open kind of question designed to deflect accusations that journalists ask loaded questions: 'How did you come to be here?'

'We were living here because the troops of the FAA came to our village and captured civilians – there were *infelicidades*.'

Infelicidades. Unhappinesses. What sort of *infelicidades*?

'They came and captured civilians – it was not the first time this happened – that's why we had to abandon our village. On the one occasion a pastor and a teacher were killed – a second time, they captured three young people who were playing ball in the field.

'The third time they captured seven people. Because they were not letting us live in peace we had to abandon our area and come here. They didn't say why they did this – they just caught people and took them away. Some were tortured.'

Joaquim introduced me to a hulk of a youth in his twenties who showed me vicious scars around his wrists from where he had been bound with wire.

'We were in the field playing ball. We met the FAA troops – we were captured and tied up.'

He told me that he and his fellow villagers had been camping out in the bush for a month now, 'eating a bit of potatoes, leaves, whatever we have'.

'Did they do this because you were helping FLEC?' I asked Joaquim.

'We weren't helping FLEC – we were people controlled by the government.'

As in Mavinga, as everywhere in Angola, so in Cabinda: being controlled by the government meant, by definition, that you couldn't be part of the enemy. Yet when I asked Joaquim what he thought of FLEC, he clammed up sooner than denounce the rebel movement.

'I don't know what to say about FLEC.'

On this first visit to Cabinda, our lodging in Cabinda town was at Simulambuco, a village just north of the city. Simulambuco features in Cabindan history as the place where the local leaders signed a treaty with the Portuguese crown, making Cabinda a Portuguese protectorate. This arrangement suited the Cabindans well enough; Portuguese protection at the time seemed to be their best defence against the ambitions of Leopold II of the Belgians, who was eyeing the whole of the Congo basin.

Cabindan nationalists still evoke Simulambuco as a touchstone of their aspirations for independence from Angola. The 1883 treaty reminds them that Cabinda was never colonised as was the rest of Angola; it had entered into a voluntary agreement with Portugal. It was only during the Salazar dictatorship in Lisbon that Cabinda was bundled into the same administrative unit as Angola. With the dictatorship overthrown in 1974, Portugal's new rulers prepared for the independence of an Angola that followed the colony's de facto borders. Cabindan liberation movements were not invited to participate in the talks leading up to Angolan independence, and the MPLA soon established its control of Cabinda's administration.

Now, 27 years later, Angolan soldiers were staying at the residential complex at Simulambuco. It was an unusual arrangement for the military to be using tourist facilities, but since the military presence outnumbered civilian visitors to Cabinda, it seemed practical to house the soldiers in the rows of little bungalows that made up the complex. As at Boavista, the cliff where it was situated appeared to be subsiding and, in the row of bungalows closest to the edge, the walls had already started to crack. The windows were small and curtained against the tropical sun, cold air blasting from air-conditioning units. Out in the bay, ChevronTexaco's oil wells were clearly visible from the grounds: the wells that provided the oil that powered the diesel generators that made the electricity that pumped cold air into the rooms. There was a selection of television channels: Angola's TPA showing government officials inaugurate hospitals in Cabinda; Portugal's RTP showing traffic reports from Lisbon; and, at night, porn movies with what little dialogue there was, mostly in Spanish.

❖

I had heard of Padre Jorge Kongo before I went to Cabinda, before I even knew the names of the various FLEC factions. He held no high office in the church, but his reputation outshone that of both the bishop and the vicar general, who were also occasionally mentioned in relation to the nationalist movement in Cabinda.

Padre Kongo looked like a man with a reputation: tall, with narrow eyes from which he peered at the world over the top of his cheekbones. At mass, in his vestments, he became a high priest. In a T-shirt (one printed by his parishioners to mark the twentieth anniversary of his ordination) he looked more like a guerrilla leader, one who remained with his people but who knew he was a rung above them in intellect and authority.

So it was to Padre Kongo that I put the definitive question that no one else had been able to answer coherently: why all this fuss about a province that is clearly no worse off than the rest of Angola? The answer began with a brief lecture on history.

'Firstly because when the MPLA arrived in Cabinda they never did anything for the future. Everything was temporary – the importation of food, done by the state in the context of a centralised economy – the very structure of the ways in which people were to survive.

'Even taking into account the economic possibilities of Cabinda, the schools to train people to work in the oil industry were set up far from Cabinda – there was never a project for the future. This is killing the people, Because of the lack of a port and an airport, imports are very expensive.'

The padre's voice now began to adopt the cadences of a sermon:

'Secondly, the hunger was a psychological hunger. Ninety-nine percent of the state budget comes from Cabinda. The war was funded from Cabinda. The excesses of the government *nomenklatura* come from Cabinda. In this way the hunger is more psychological than physical – it is different from the hunger of Moxico, Huambo or Luanda.'

The claim about the origins of the state revenue was exaggerated – in reality, Cabinda provides some 80 percent of Angola's income – but the point Padre Kongo was making was obvious enough. In a sense, the padre had no choice but to explain Cabinda in this way, using terms like 'psychological hunger' rather than speaking of unqualified misery. He knew what Angola was like, that there was more to Angola than venal rulers growing fat on Cabindan oil and that, in fact, the average non-Cabindan Angolan was rather worse off than the average Cabindan. Those Cabindans who had never left their little corridor of rainforest and coastal scrub had no such insight. Young men from the seminary next to Kongo's church would greet visitors, without a flicker of irony, with the words: *'Bem-vindo no nosso país de sofrimento'* – Welcome to our country of suffering.

What set the Cabindans aside from the Angolans was how they responded to their *sofrimento*. Unlike the people of Boavista, the Cabindans would never pack their bags and do what the government told them to do nor channel their anger into throwing stones at cats. Nor would the Cabindans sprinkle their speech with subjunctives when they talked about the strange and alien hypothesis of peace, as the people in the *deslocado* camps and UNITA quartering areas of Moxico had done. Cabindans would sometimes talk about *confusão*, but seldom about *situação*; that concept was too fatalistic for them.

Angolans had spent their lives watching other Angolans wage war, watching other Angolans exploit and imprison and kill, whether as government or as rebels. No experience in a quarter-century of self-rule had been able to persuade Angolans that things could be any different. Angolan jokes went along the following lines: 'When God made Angola, he gave it diamonds, oil, all the minerals you can imagine; he gave it fertile land and a wonderful climate; he gave Angola beautiful mountains and beaches, and an ocean full of fish. Then he looked at what he had created and thought, "It's not fair that one country can have so much bounty." So to compensate, God made Angolans.'

Cabindans did not bother with that kind of self-deprecating humour. Their way of distancing themselves from a generation of misrule was to deny they were Angolans at all. The sliver of Congo that separated them from the other 17 provinces was an obvious

145

pillar of their argument, and the Simulambuco treaty, for those who could be bothered to trace the historical intricacies, was a more delicate but also more polemically convincing one. There was no legal political movement, however, through which they might express such separatist convictions. So instead they went to church.

Even at 6.30 on a weekday morning, the Mission Church would be full for the dawn mass, those who could not get seats clustering around the doors. Afterwards, Padre Kongo would pass among the faithful, blessing the packets of candles that the women had brought along. No one else in Cabinda could have convened a crowd of such a size; elsewhere in Angola such gatherings happened only if the National Spontaneous Movement had a hand in the organisation.

Another event, some time after my first visit, even more amply illustrated the pulling power of Catholicism: the centenary of the church in Lândana, the first sizable town on the road north of the provincial capital. Much of Cabinda's population seemed to have descended on Lândana on the Saturday when the event was celebrated. The spiky pink church, which sits above the town overlooking the mangrove-lined beach, had just been renovated. The main road through the town was closed to vehicles, and stalls selling beer, peanuts, *frango no churrasco* (grilled chicken) were crammed against each other for the entire length of the street. The town was full of people on foot, in priestly vestments, Boy Scout gear, Sunday best, or T-shirts printed with an image of the church on the front and corporate logos, including that of ChevronTexaco, on the back.

ChevronTexaco had picked up much of the bill for the church's renovation – part of the 'social investment' programme that the government had written into every foreign oil company's operating contract. But it was the diocese, not the government, that had persuaded ChevronTexaco to plough its cash into rebuilding one large early twentieth century church. In effect, the church had acquired the ability to extract taxes.

I asked one of the priests how he felt about accepting money from a company that was so despised.

'It's our petroleum, it's our money.'

The Cabindan priests were loathed by the government in Luanda. Once, after I had written an article about a report on human rights abuses that the fathers had put together, the presidential spokesman Aldemiro Vaz de Conceição had phoned me, hissing with rage: '*Os padres são de FLEC*' (the fathers are from FLEC). The church, however, continued regardless to do what it wanted to do. Travelling through areas where the FAA had only recently been on the hunt for FLEC, it was clear to me that the label 'Diocese de Cabinda' on the side of our white air-conditioned double-cab bakkie was a talisman against the FAA as well as FLEC. Government soldiers at roadblocks waved us through, occasionally in exchange for a ride on the back for a couple of kilometres. Our driver was a red-haired *mestiço*, which in Cabinda meant that the authorities would either assume he was with the government or not take him seriously at all.

Cabinda's priests handed out food and clothes to displaced people where the government had failed to do so. Young men in search of a cheap higher education could get it at the seminary whether or not they intended to join the clergy – were they all to have graduated, Cabinda would have found itself exporting more priests than petroleum.

If UNITA had, in the further reaches of the *terras ao fim do mundo*, behaved more like a huge and mobile state than a rebel movement, in Cabinda it was the church that had become the rival to the state. Kongo and the rest of them were like the turbulent priests of mediaeval Europe, defying king and court in Luanda and their demand for tribute from that distant province.

If the government hesitated to raise its sword against the priests, it had no such scruples when it came to the peasants. The Cabindan mantra '*país de sofrimento*' may not have borne much relation to the standard of living in the province, but when 30 000 troops arrived, the Cabindans genuinely had something to complain about. The presence of the troops seemed like the proof that Cabindans wanted that they were living under an occupying power. Particularly when the soldiers accused Cabindan peasants of helping 'your brothers in FLEC' and castigated girls as 'FLEC women' when they raped them.

By the early months of 2003, it had become clear what was going on.

Tina, aged 15, sat on the terrace at the Catholic presbytery, twisting the strap of her imitation snakeskin bag as she told her story. No one knew how many soldiers had raped her. Her voice was a monotone; her fingers never stopped moving.

'They came to get me, and I tried to run away. He said "If you run away, I'll kill you." They took me to the barracks, sent me to a room there. He pushed me onto the bed, and started beating me. He started beating me on the chest, with his pistol, and said "Today I'm going to fuck you." Then he said, "Today I'll send 15 soldiers to have fun." He called me "woman from FLEC" and sent someone to fetch a machete. He said: "It's been a long time since I killed anyone."'

Tina survived to tell her story. André Bazi's daughters did not.

I was glad to be able to record André's rambling account, Ibinda words scattered throughout his speech, so as to confirm the details afterwards. Normally, when you cannot understand everything that is said first time round, it is at least possible to respond to an interviewee's tone of voice, gestures, expressions without leading the narrative astray by assuming the role of counsellor, but André spoke with so little obvious emotion that I wasn't sure when to nod in agreement, compassion, or encouragement. I had to listen again to the recording to make certain that I had heard the impassive testimony of a man talking of the violent death of both his children.

'The troops arrived in our area and occupied our houses forcibly. We found ourselves living among them. They stayed for a week, eating in our houses. My daughters cooked for them, served them very well.'

This domestic relationship, even if it was an involuntary one, meant that André had developed a certain confidence in the soldiers. When his daughters went on an errand to the next village, it did not bother him that they set off along the same path where the soldiers had recently gone. As he learnt later from some women who had been working in the fields, one of the soldiers broke away from the group he was with and walked back along the path towards where the girls were.

'The soldier caught up with my younger girl. He fired three shots. The older one tried to run away – he killed her, three shots again.'

Like André, Pedro Nzau Paulo was not used to giving interviews. He was, after all, a peasant farmer whose main concern was usually a matter of coaxing enough manioc out of the ground to keep his family plugged up with starch throughout the year. Now he looked weary and broken.

'I left the house about nine o'clock to go to my fields. In the field I ran into soldiers who were on operations. They made me go with them.'

Pedro recalled being forced to march with the soldiers for two days. They had asked him things about FLEC to which, not being a soldier, he had been unable to respond. As a result he had been tied up and 'beaten with a very big torture'.

He showed the nick in his ear and the scars on his arms from the ropes.

'They tied me up fast, arms and legs, and started to beat me till I passed out. When I came around, I saw the troops.

'Then they tied me up by my testicles – the commandant pulled the rope, hauled me up.'

Pedro was kept captive by the troops for eight days, and spent a further four days at their barracks before being released.

'Everything was damaged from they way they tied me up. I lost my strength from the way they tied me up – I have no way of working, no way of supporting my children.'

Tina, André and Pedro had told me their stories in the course of a trip to Cabinda that I made in February 2003 with Rafael Marques and Justino Pinto de Andrade, who were collecting testimonies of human rights abuses. We were unable to get out of the city; the Cabindan activists had been unable on this occasion to organise safe conduct for obvious foreigners, but they had organised for people to come from the north of the province to talk to us. Tina's parish priest had come from Buco Zau and offered a new technique for long-distance war reporting: he had brought along a mini cassette recorder. He was able to treat us to a tape of explosions, made no less impressive by the tinny sound coming from the speakers.

'They were bombing from 9.30 at night until 5.00 in the morning.'

Our trip to Cabinda took place over a weekend, and on Sunday we went to Padre Kongo's mass at the Catholic Mission Church on the waterfront. The mass was sung in Ibinda, ebbing and flowing in a mode that seemed alternately major and minor, like blues, with a rhythmic percussive chime that kept insistently to the same note as the singing surged around it. Padre Kongo was in full flight, welcoming home two parishioners who had been detained without trial and recently released. He spoke alternately in Ibinda and Portuguese. There was, admittedly, a white Portuguese man in the congregation, a businessman who had just been appointed to the parish council. But it was hard to put aside the thought that Kongo's excursions into Portuguese might be for the benefit of us visitors, and for anyone else from outside who might be listening.

'The Angolan government has to recognise that FLEC is the only representative of the people of Caaa ...'

'Cabinda!' roared the congregation, on cue.

Later, I got to talk to the two men who had been released from detention. The first – let us call him Zé – was in his forties but looked older, delicate and slightly hunched. The soldiers had come for him at home early in December, when he had gone to lie down after feeling a fever coming on. He spent two days in a cell at the barracks in town. By the end of that time he had full-blown malaria and was examined at a military hospital. The nurse, he recalled, had insisted that he stay and receive treatment. The soldiers ignored her and took him away, not to a cell this time. They put him in a pit in the ground full of insects, scorpions and rainwater; there he had spent most of the five weeks he was in detention.

A day after his release he was taken back to the cells and passed from military to civilian courts. He was still unsure of his legal status.

The other detainee – I shall call him Joaquim – was larger and stronger than his colleague, and had had a less harrowing time. He had simply been detained at a roadblock, and held for eight days in a tiny, dirty storeroom at the military headquarters, unable to contact his family.

Joaquim freely admitted to having been, as he put it, 'a guerrilla man' (he was also a ChevronTexaco employee and could speak reasonably good English) until 1983. Later on, he had been part of a FLEC civilian committee in the town, which he said was trying to promote talks between the government and the rebels. Justino asked him if he still considered himself a collaborator. The answer was telling.

'If I am a FLEC collaborator, then the whole population of Cabinda are FLEC collaborators.'

When I returned to Cabinda towards the end of 2003, the fence surrounding the ChevronTexaco compound had started to blossom with the little red triangular signs that I had first seen in Luena, before Savimbi died: the signs that indicate a minefield. The mines were not new, as I discovered when I phoned the ChevronTexaco office in Luanda. The company spokesman said there had been a minefield inside the perimeter fence for some 20 years, dating from the era when Gulf Oil operated under Cuban protection. It was only now that the company had seen fit to put up the warning signs. The spokesman said it was the government's responsibility to remove the mines, when it saw fit.

It looked as if they would be there for a long time to come.

9

Diamonds and charcoal

Cafunfo was built on diamonds, yet much of the population seemed to live from selling charcoal: a dual economy built on carbon in its most precious and its most workaday molecular forms. The town lay at the heart of the Cuango River valley of Angola's north-east, a place that in the 1990s had produced most of the diamonds that funded UNITA's war.

Each afternoon a procession of men and women would make its way up the hill from the river back to the town, the women carrying bundles of wood or baskets of manioc tubers, the men with shovels and sieves made out of old car radiators. Now, in 2003, that was still the system here in the Lunda region, Angola's richest diamond-producing area – the men would spend month after month sifting through river gravel. Maybe, if they were lucky, they might find a diamond once a year. The women in the family would burn charcoal and grow manioc – two substances of similar nutritional value – to keep them alive in the far more likely event that no diamonds appeared among the gravel.

The road that diamond diggers and charcoal burners and manioc farmers followed for part of the way at Cafunfo was cut by an erosion gully that was within metres of slicing through the airport runway on which we landed – in one of the Antonovs run by a general. Cafunfo was not on the state airline's schedule. The US$100-ticket it cost to get there, a photocopied slip of paper, looked as though it would be barely valid on a small-town bus service. But after we had waited for half an hour in a cloud of mosquitoes in the 4.00 a.m. pre-dawn at Luanda airport's domestic terminal, someone opened a side-gate leading directly onto the airport apron and we were allowed to board, stumbling up the vehicle ramp at the back of the plane. Seats with tattered scarlet and green upholstery had been bolted to the floor of the transport plane; there were no portholes.

An hour or so later we were at Cafunfo, a mess of cinderblock buildings scattered over the red earth. In this town of diamonds, the streets were made of garbage. The litter, for once, had a purpose: people would pack bags of rubbish into the ravines that the heavy summer rain scoured out of the streets, the idea being to dam up the mud and slow down the erosion. Flimsy carrier bags, tins, discarded hair extensions all protruded from the matrix of mud that was the road. There were no schools beyond the fourth grade. There used to be a health post, but it had been converted into a police station.

The shops were larger concrete boxes that looked as though they ought to be selling plastic buckets or candles – something mundane, though necessary in a place without electricity or running water. In fact, the shops existed not to sell things, but to buy diamonds. They were distinguished only by their signs; the dealers' names were picked out in mirror tiles to look like diamond facets. One of the signs bore the name of Tchatchumbala, a souvenir of Cafunfo's UNITA days.

The old truism about the war in Angola was that the government had the oil, but UNITA had the diamonds. The part about the oil was true; the offshore location of Angola's oil wells ensured that the government controlled who drilled and how the profits were divided up. Diamonds were more complicated. The gems were to be found in just about every province of the Angolan interior, mixed in with stones of lesser value in the riverbeds. There had never been a time when one or other political faction commanded all of Angola's diamonds. UNITA's share of the diggings had flowed and ebbed with its fortunes on the battlefield. In contrast to the oil industry, where each new drilling site needed years of research and millions of dollars before the first litre of black ooze reached the surface, many of Angola's diamonds were there for the taking. Controlling the diamonds was no more complicated than controlling the people who scratched them out of the earth.

Mavinga, in the far south-east, was a long way from the Lundas, but the rules were the same. On one trip there six months after the end of the war, I had found the Capembe and Matungo rivers near the two UNITA quartering areas crowded with people. The women were doing the laundry, and the men were digging for diamonds, hacking out the grey mud with picks and spades; the young boys would then sift the gravel for diamonds.

UNITA's control of such backyard diamond diggings across the country had doubtless contributed its share to Savimbi's coffers, and the biggest concentration of diamonds was in the provinces of Lunda Norte and Lunda Sul. It was, above all, by capturing diamond fields in these two provinces that UNITA had managed to keep funding a war after 1992.

I first got a clue as to what was happening in the Lundas when Panzo, a Cabindan who had worked there during the war, showed me the scar on his calf 'where the commandos shot us with an AKM when they saw the diamonds'. Much of his work had involved diving for diamonds in the rivers – or sometimes diving for the bodies of less skilled divers: 'Tongues out like this, eyes out like this – sometimes they had been in the river for four days before we pulled them out.'

Panzo had worked in a world where UNITA and government constantly exchanged control of land and mining rights, where foreign dealers paid $250 to military officers for prospecting rights. 'Lots of Senegalese, Malians, Cape Verdeans, Nigerians, Lebanese – they don't speak Portuguese, they don't have the papers, but they are there in the Lundas.'

In 1998, the return of these fields to government control signalled the beginning of the end for Savimbi's movement. At the same time, the United Nations had promoted sanctions aimed at preventing the sale of diamonds from the areas that UNITA still controlled. The civil war in Sierra Leone, and to a lesser extent the one in Angola, ensured that the term 'conflict diamonds' entered the vocabulary of the world's media, and, in the last years of the century, sanctions against 'conflict diamonds' had succeeded in reducing, if not eliminating, the trade between rebel fighters and the rest of the world.

By the 1990s, there was no question of the Angolan war being about ideology or about anybody's freedom. It was about money. Analysts have used the term 'resource war' to describe this very contemporary kind of conflict. In spirit, though, a resource war shares much with a system characterised as 'primitive extraction' – a term that the historian Basil Davidson, writing in the 1960s, used to describe the early days of the colonial economy in Angola. Colonial officials were free to grab what they wanted from the earth or from the people of the conquered territory, provided that they rendered a predetermined tax to the Portuguese crown each year. Wartime Angola echoed the colonial past. The FAA generals who won back territory from UNITA could do more or less what they liked with it, as long as enough of a cut went back to Luanda. When it suited them, government and UNITA generals would trade with each other.

Tchatchumbala – the name on the shop sign in Cafunfo – was a Congolese man who had been responsible for much of the trade with UNITA in the days when Savimbi's men controlled Cafunfo and the rest of the Cuango valley. When UNITA was driven out of Cafunfo in 1998, Tchatchumbala had disappeared for a while. Now he was back. The opportunities to make money were the same, whichever army may have been controlling the area. The people in the Cuango also seemed to think it made little difference whether the government or UNITA was in charge.

Dressed in the *soba* (traditional chief) uniform of long khakis and peaked military cap, Sousa Kandonda Kononoko took the floor at a community meeting in Cuango town.

'When UNITA left we thought there would be peace,' he grumbled. The rest of the people assembled there tutted and clucked in deferential agreement.

AN OUTBREAK OF PEACE

'After two weeks under the control of the government we heard that SDM had arrived. Not much later, Alfa 5 shot someone dead, near the river. We don't know why – probably because he was on the road by himself and suspected of stealing diamonds. People can't even go to the river any more.'

SDM – Sociedade de Desenvolvimento Mineiro de Angola – was a commercial diamond mining company, owned partly by the Angolan state diamond company, Endiama, and partly by the Brazilian firm Odebrecht. Driving south of Cafunfo, one saw for hours signboards marking SDM's concession lands in the dense woodlands. Alfa 5 was the private security company contracted by several of the mining firms in the Lundas. Founded by former high-ranking officers in the FAA, it drew on the skills of the South African mercenary company Executive Outcomes, which the Angolan government had employed to push UNITA out of the diamond fields in the 1990s.

After the end of the war, the symbiosis continued: the government granted the diamond concessions to its favoured partners, the white mercenary officers were in charge of security, the guards themselves were FAA soldiers. Or, rather, former FAA soldiers now in private employment. The peasants and diamond diggers who complained about their activities did not seem to know or care about the difference between a soldier and a security guard. For them, not much had changed since the days when people like Panzo scratched out their diamonds in the space between two warring armies. Private companies now went about their business with the unchecked authority of the military in battle. But the diamond buyers in Antwerp and Tel Aviv no longer had to worry about complying with sanctions. The diamonds were now legal since they were no longer conflict diamonds – how could they be conflict diamonds when there was, officially, no more conflict?

After the *soba*, a woman got up to speak about how security guards had destroyed her fields when SDM moved into the lands which she farmed: 'We asked for compensation but they gave us nothing. The least we are asking for is for our husbands and sons to be given jobs. Now our only means of survival is burning charcoal.'

Said another man: 'The diamonds are the property of the people of Lunda Norte. All we of the east are ex-combatants, yet we don't have the right to mine. Those of us who fought in the south never brought back a head of cattle or a bag of maize from the south.'

❖

Stories went around in the Lundas about how early foreign travellers had found mud huts decorated with shiny stones – stones that had no intrinsic value other than decoration since they were never traded outside of the region. The act of digging diamonds out of river gravel has a name in Angola: *garimpo*. A practitioner of *garimpo* is a *garimpeiro*.

'In Lunda Norte *garimpo* is part of family life, part of the fabric of society,' said one of the region's few foreign aid workers, who had spent years in the Lundas. 'Everyone has a few diamonds.'

As diamonds acquired cash value, *garimpo* ceased to be just a way of decorating one's house, and came to form the bottom tier of a multi-layered industry. The next rung involved a more sophisticated way of getting diamonds out of the mud: dredging with machines to extract and sieve the gravel, the domain of army generals whose concessions were the spoils of the post-1992 war. Then there was open-cast mining: mechanical diggers and trucks that cleared earth from a vast area, the sifting and sorting done by machine. The investment required in such an operation necessitated the involvement of big business.

That was where the likes of SDM came in. Elsewhere in the Lundas, other companies under different names linked Endiama to partners from South Africa, Portugal, Israel and Britain. The global diamond giant De Beers was not there. Relations between De Beers and the government had been sour ever since the corporation had bought diamonds from UNITA in the early 1990s. De Beers retained representatives in Luanda, but occasional rumours that it was about to reach a mutually acceptable deal with the government had, thus far, proved unfounded.

As international corporations jostled for their share of Angola's diamonds, people in the Lundas complained that they were allowed into the industry only at the humblest level, living the precarious existence of *garimpeiros*, or as menial labourers working the mines or the dredgers. When it came to buying and selling the diamonds, their prospects were no better. At the end of the 1990s, the government had set up a company called Ascorp to channel the money that was supposed to start flooding in from diamond fields that were no longer in the fiefdom of UNITA.

Ascorp would issue licences to dealers in the principal diamond-producing centres, conferring on them the sole legal right to buy from the *garimpeiros* – and obliging them to sell on to Ascorp. Just under half of Ascorp was owned by an Israeli-Ukrainian magnate called Lev Leviev and a Belgian corporation called Omega; the other 51 percent belonged to the Angolan state, or possibly to individuals closely connected to the state. No one in the industry seemed entirely sure. Transactions took place in cash dollars; auditing was no more evident in the diamond industry than in the oil industry.

It was Ascorp that had issued licences to the dealers who had their names displayed in mirror tiles on the shops in Cafunfo. The names were seldom Angolan.

'They have room for Senegalese and Congolese – not Angolans,' complained a group of men in Cafunfo's waterlogged market.

'Aren't Angolans allowed to work for Ascorp?' I asked.

The response was a raucous chorus of 'No!'

The Senegalese men would sit in the front yards of their houses, or simply hang around on street corners looking for business. I approached one of them, asking him what he did in Cafunfo; he spoke no Portuguese, and replied in French.

'*Je suis debrouilleur.*' A great French word: I'm someone who gets by, figures things out, finds a way.

But how did he come to be in Angola?

'God created Africa for the Africans. The Angolans also believe Africa is for the Africans.'

This made me curious to know how he knew what the Angolans believed, since his ignorance of Portuguese and of any indigenous languages must have made communication difficult. How did he manage to converse?

'Je me debrouille.' I get by. I figure things out.

Such taciturn responses made it difficult to figure out exactly how foreigners had been allowed such a role in the informal side of the diamond trade in Angola. The locals saw it as part of a conspiracy: if the local Lunda-Chokwe people were allowed to become a force within the industry, they might start insisting that some of the diamond money be spent on providing running water to Cafunfo, for a start.

'They keep people oppressed so they can't claim their socio-economic rights,' was Dr António Buyamba's view on the matter. The doctor's home and consulting room were another squat concrete box on another lane made of mud and garbage. Towards the end of the day two young Congolese, all peaked hair and gold chains, arrived at the surgery. They were not in search of medical attention. They had diamonds, and they were in search of a buyer. The doctor, it appeared, did a bit of dealing on the side, even if he was not in the league of Tchatchumbala.

In the Lundas as in Cabinda, people would make an article of faith out of being deprived of the riches of the area where they lived. In Cabinda, the mismatch between what the region produced and what it received was goading people to call for independence. In the Lundas, the same mismatch had given rise to a political party. It was called the Partido de Renovação Social (Social Renewal Party, the PRS). It had won five parliamentary seats in the 1992 election, which put it in third place. A long way behind the MPLA and UNITA, for sure, but what was significant was it scored the best election result out of all of the new parties that emerged in 1992, products of that first rush towards democracy which did not owe their place at the table to their former status as armed guerrilla movements. The PRS had, in fact, done slightly better than the third of the old independence movements, Holden Roberto's FNLA. It did well by going where party politics had never gone before in Angola.

The PRS had taken root among a people who since the 1960s had watched three parties, each identified with one or other far-off region of the country, battle it out for control of the whole lot. Driving through the Lundas, you would as likely see the PRS flag, a white circle on a red, green and black background, flying above the mango trees of a village as you would see the yellow star of the MPLA. This meant that the *soba* of that village had joined the PRS; in a society where political loyalty had become so linked to political control, this was important. Yet activists campaigned at their own risk. Dr Buyamba was the local secretary of the party; he showed me gory snapshots of three party members who had been shot dead in the space of six months.

Joaquim Nafoia, the party's secretary for youth affairs, was making a tour of the Lundas. At a meeting in a Cafunfo schoolroom, he lectured his audience on the roots of their own deprivation, drawing them in before the end of each sentence, so as to let them fill in the right word. 'The wealth of this region is being ... stolen. The diamonds should be used for the benefit of the ... people.' Although he was now based at the party headquarters in Luanda, the Lundas were home to Nafoia as they were to most of the party's leadership. He would boast how, when out campaigning, he needed no bed; he was happy to sleep seated at a table, his head resting on his folded arms.

Walking around the garbage-mat of the lanes in Cafunfo, Nafoia shook his head at the way that local girls had started wearing the kind of miniskirts and crop tops that were standard dress for women under 40 in Luanda. 'That's the Western style, isn't it?' he asked me. In truth, it was a style of dress that I associated with Angola more than anywhere else.

Late one night we arrived in a small town, where Nafoia headed straight to the building that was the party's local office and found the local secretary. We sat around a table by candlelight. Nafoia asked how many people were doing *garimpo* in the area – what problems they had encountered – whether the mining companies were encroaching on anyone's land. The local secretary hesitated and ummed – Nafoia scolded him.

'To be an effective activist you must make it your duty to know these things.'

I asked the secretary about the recent history of the town.

'The enemy attacked in 1997 and 1999, but didn't take it back,' the man began. Nafoia interrupted impatiently again.

'Why are you referring to UNITA as "the enemy"? *Os dois são bandidos.*' (The MPLA and UNITA are both bandits).

All of this was workaday political campaigning by the standards of most countries. Yet here in Angola it was a revelation to see a party mobilising people by engaging with the realities of their lives, rather than counting on their support as the consequence of loyalties forged in the civil war.

Nafoia and his comrades spoke with an almost religious reverence about their king – King Muatchissengue wa Tembo, paramount chief of the Angolan half of the Lunda-Chokwe kingdom that extended north into the Democratic Republic of Congo. They took me to meet him in Itengo, a village of brown mud houses much like any other, where he held court on a throne woven out of wood and bark placed by his courtiers on a worn lion skin in front of the cracked walls of his house. The king emerged in his broad-brimmed hat, shirt and tie and tweed jacket, and a billowing red skirt: a shrunken man, white-bearded with steely eyes and a knowing smile. The men of the village sat in a circle on plastic garden chairs while the king pronounced on the state of the kingdom.

'Look where I'm living.' He gestured from his throne to the dilapidated house. 'They talk about the wealth of their region. The people from this region from where thousands of carats are coming don't know where these riches are going.

'We are being colonised by black Angolans. We were already colonised by the Portuguese. Now this is worse.'

The women sat on the ground to one side. His Majesty explained how women were always able to participate in the decisions of his court: they participated as observers. Later, when I left my chair, walked over and crouched down on the earth to solicit some views from the ladies of the court, I was greeted with mild concern from the men, and incredulous giggles from the women themselves.

As we drove away from Itengo, the PRS people turned up the volume as a crackly tape played on the stereo, laughing and cheering at the lyrics that were in the Chokwe language. This was the best music, they pointed out – not that *kizomba* stuff from the coast. I didn't particularly like the music, but the insistent jangle was in itself less depressing than the realisation that the fervour of people like Nafoia – however much they might profess to have Angolan interests at heart – came down to nothing more than regional sentiment, nostalgia for an imagined tradition, and a sneering suspicion of anyone from elsewhere in Angola. No one in the Lundas spoke of independence the way the Cabindans did, but the conviction was equally strong of being oppressed not by a few powerful individuals, but by people from a different place. The response in the Lundas was to scorn everything that came from elsewhere. Their king, their music and their culture were better than the degenerate creoles of the coast. Their diamonds were better than the cattle and maize of the south.

The following week, back in Luanda, I met a human rights activist who was visiting from Swaziland. We started talking about what was going on in the Lundas and the people I had met; then I stopped short, wondering how to explain to this woman, whose work was directed at bringing democracy to Africa's last absolute monarchy, how it was that in the Lundas the best alternative they could present was an octogenarian hereditary leader.

Nzaji, in the east of Lunda Norte, looked like an American suburb from the movies: avenues lined with flowering trees, bungalows with wide verandas, children playing on the lawns that ran down to the traffic-free roads. There was even electricity – there was a hydroelectric dam on the Luachimbo River in Dundo, not far away, and even though only one of the four turbines was still functioning, it provided light for all the surrounding towns.

It was a Sunday, and we stopped outside the Evangelical church to talk to the *garimpeiros* as they left the service.

'When doing *garimpo* you have to stay very alert,' said a youth dressed in a dark suit and clutching a black-covered Bible. But for a few threads of beard, he looked no more than 13. 'If someone says the security is coming, you have to run. If you are caught they put you in jail, and to get out you have to pay $50.' (Just as all diamond transactions were done in cash American dollars, so the police would expect greenbacks rather than local currency as a bribe.)

'The security use the *garimpeiros* for their intelligence because we know where the best places are for diamonds,' the young man continued. 'They push us further and further from the town. Then we go to a new place. Sometimes we have to walk 80 kilometres to the river.'

The men kept at it because there was nothing else to do.

'There's no work, so I've been doing *garimpo* since I came out of the army six years ago,' said a man called Franklin. 'If you find something, you might get $100 or $200 – it depends on the diamond. If not, you starve. I know some *garimpeiros* who have gone five years without finding anything.'

Nzaji's suburban bungalows were reserved for civil servants and diamond dealers. The *garimpeiros* lived in self-built box houses just like the ones in Cafunfo. Here, too, the soil was eroding rapidly, and the townships crowded worryingly close to the edge of ravines. A long, cathedral-high building in the town had once been the largest vehicle assembly plant in Africa outside of South Africa. Now it was empty: a town that had once been the centre of a mining and industrial region extending into the former Belgian Congo was now an isolated dead-end.

A green hill at Nzaji's edge held a sizable hospital. A doctor showed me the facilities: the echoing operating theatre, bare except for a table in the very centre, and a metal wardrobe at the side; this the doctor opened to show a white operating gown, stained and worn to rags. With the anaesthetic machine no longer working, surgery in this theatre was performed by injecting the patient with ketamine, much as UNITA had done in its grass-thatch hospitals in the bush. The theatre, at least, was clean. In the wards, the windows were broken and cobwebs hung low above the patients' heads.

The houses, the hydroelectric station, the factory, the hospital – the remnants of a sophisticated town – were the work not of the colonial administration, but of a commercial enterprise. While the

Cafunfo diamond rush had begun not long before independence, and its history had always been woven into that of the civil war, here in the east of Lunda Norte the industry had started earlier and had had time to grow. Commercial diamond mining was said to have begun with the discovery of seven diamonds in a river in 1912. Five years later, Diamang was established with its headquarters in Dundo. The company was owned partly by the Portuguese state, and partly by private interests in Britain and Belgium, both of them countries that already had substantial mining ventures in southern and central Africa.

Diamonds became Angola's most valuable export, until they were overtaken by coffee at mid-century and, later, by petroleum. Diamang was answerable not to Luanda, but directly to Lisbon; the colonial administration had in any case come late to this part of the country and the corporation became something akin to a state in itself, its responsibilities extending beyond diamonds to secondary industry, housing, education and health care. In Lucapa, another of the old mining towns, Diamang had built a mining college where local people could receive training to work in the industry. It had closed some time in the 1980s, and the skilled labour now came from elsewhere.

This is not to say that Diamang was ever a benevolent employer. Substantial portions of its workforce had been provided through 'the intervention of the authorities' – forced labour, in other words – and in the 1950s the colonial government, fearing an uprising, had ordered the company to double the wages of its black employees. Yet the present had truncated memories of the past. With no faith in the government, people looked to Endiama – Diamang's successor – as the provider.

I listened to two civil servants speak, sitting on the heavy sofas around the coffee table in one of the American houses.

'The mining companies ought to build schools, medical posts, and houses,' said one of the men.

He had lived all his life under corporate rule. The thought that these tasks might be the duty of the government did not seem to have occurred to him.

❖

If Angolans wanted to see any benefit from the land's diamond wealth, the best they could do was to bypass the law and the machinations of the state and its proxies. A few individuals managed to find a place in this backdoor trade – far from the Lundas, on the Namibian border.

South of the border, at Namibia's northern edge, lies a dusty expanse of strip-malls and supermarkets known as Rundu, with shop names like 'Amigo Wholesalers' and *kizomba* music pumping from loudspeakers giving a clue to the nationality of the customers the stores are targeting. Visible on the other side of the Kavango River – or the Cubango as the Angolans call it – a sky-blue police station and pink administrative buildings mark out the town of Calai as unmistakeably Angolan. Those pink buildings are matched by the new pink Angolan consulate on the Namibian side of the river. There is no official border post here, though a raft-like ferry will take you back and forth between the two countries.

The trader was hanging around outside the pink consulate. He did business with South Africa, he explained. He was paid by a man in Cape Town to bring diamonds from Angola.

'Where do you get the diamonds from,' I asked.

'Near Mavinga.'

I remembered the UNITA men digging diamonds at the Capembe quartering area more than two years earlier; the government had long ago promised to put a stop to such operations, so I was curious to hear whether they were still going on.

'Capembe?' I asked the dealer.

'Yes, Capembe. I buy the diamonds from the UNITA people there.'

'Where do you cross the border?' I asked the trader.

'I don't cross the border. I get the ferry. When I am this side, I speak English, I am Namibian. When I am that side, I speak Portuguese, I am Angolan.'

Two days later, in Menongue, the provincial capital, I asked the deputy provincial governor of Cuando Cubango about the state of the diamond industry in the province.

'There is no diamond mining in Cuando Cubango,' he stated. 'The industry has not yet been rehabilitated.'

10

Life in a time of peace

Luanda greeted the new year with a new police force. The *fiscais* (fiscal police) appeared on the streets in January 2003, their khaki shirts making them look more like private security guards than officers of the law. Their main purpose was apparently to harass the *zungueiras*, those women who spent their lives tramping through the streets of the city centre, carrying on their head a basket of merchandise: often fruit, vegetables or fish, but also clothes, shoes, insecticide sprays, bottles of liquor, or loaves of bread and tinned *choriço* to make sandwiches. In the past they had moved at a stately pace appropriate to someone carrying 20 kilograms or more on her head. Now, it had become quite normal to see a woman running at a steady trot with one hand raised to make sure her basket stayed put. This sight usually meant the *fiscais* were following not far behind.

Getting caught was costly. One young woman in the Baixa told me the police had fined her 200 kwanzas – about three dollars at the prevailing exchange rate – and also confiscated the pineapples she was selling, which would have earned her about ten dollars. Thirteen dollars would have meant about a week's profits; a *zungueira* was frequently the only breadwinner in her family. (That same month, the national airline's in-flight magazine had an illustrated feature on the *zungueiras* and how important they were to the life and to the traditions of the city.)

The teenage boys who lived in the backyards of the middle-class blocks of flats, and survived by running errands and washing cars, were doing no better. The *fiscais* deemed it illegal to wash a car in the street, even though few car owners in this built-up part of town had a place where they could wash their vehicle away from the street. In any case, it was the boys and not the owners who suffered the consequences. Agostinho told how he had been apprehended while washing a car, and taken to the *fiscais'* headquarters. They demanded money which he did not have; eventually he was released in return for washing the police commander's own car.

The provincial government's demolition squads had been at work over the Christmas season as well, knocking down more than a thousand owner-occupied houses in the Soba Kapassa *bairro*. Residents like Engracia André were still wondering why. Looking more bewildered than angry, she said: 'We are very concerned because so far no one has offered an explanation as to why this happened, or what is to become of us.' 'Us' included her daughter, mother, and two orphaned nephews who had lived in the same house.

Her neighbour, Martins António, felt betrayed. He had always been a loyal MPLA activist: 'These are the people who were elected to govern us, and then they do things that just aren't right.'

It had become a truism to say how the end of the war in Angola had opened up new opportunities for democracy and human rights. It was with this in mind that Sérgio Vieira de Mello, the United Nations High Commissioner for Human Rights, was visiting Angola. The UN Human Rights Division had invited the press corps to accompany the high commissioner on a day-trip to Malange.

Two ten-seater Beechcraft were waiting at the airport: one for the journalists, and the other for the UN people, presumably so the high commissioner would not have to sit next to a journalist. The UN party had not yet arrived, though, and we killed time on the tarmac as the morning started to grow hot. Parked near the Beechcraft was an oddly shaped single-engine propeller plane, painted in camouflage. A visiting French cameraman asked what it was.

'That was the plane that killed Savimbi,' said one veteran gravel-voiced, chain-smoking Angolan hack who worked for Portuguese television.

This, apparently, was the reconnaissance aircraft that had helped to track Savimbi down in Moxico – a Brazilian model called a Tucano. It did have the look of an ungainly jungle bird about it.

The journalist nodded towards the Tucano: 'There's 70 million dollars on the ground now. Savimbi died because he had no more money. The MPLA won because it had money.'

Waiting for takeoff, we looked over to the Antonovs and Ilyushins that now sat heavily on the runway – planes that had helped to make generals millionaires during the war. I thought back to just over a year ago and the soldier speaking to a woman trader getting onto the plane: 'When the war ends, you'll go by car.'

At Malange, where I had last been six months earlier when the Red Cross took young Miguel and António to be reunited with their families, a signboard at the airport announced a 'rehabilitation programme'. The building still looked shattered, but they were painting the control tower pink. A convoy of a dozen white four-by-fours was there to meet us, a passenger list pasted to each windscreen. We headed out of town for about 20 kilometres, with what must have been the entire Malange traffic police force lining the route and making the appropriate hand signals when we turned off the main road on to the dirt track leading to the resettlement centre that the government had selected as De Mello's rural experience.

Quite apart from the sudden influx of traffic cops and little paper-chains made from school exercise books hanging from the bushes, the resettlement centre seemed a lot better off than any IDP settlement I had seen in Angola. It had a brick-built school building, and a vast shady mulemba tree, like a naturally occurring *jango*, where the villagers had assembled to meet the high commissioner. De Mello did his spiel about being here not to talk, but to listen. The people gave the white man in his white car plenty to listen to.

'*Não temos peixe! Não temos sal! Não temos sabão! Sofremos bué!*'

(We don't have fish! We don't have salt! We don't have soap! We're suffering a lot!)

On the way back to Malange, while a colossal thunderstorm hurled bucket after bucket of water at the windscreen, a local UN official spoke ruefully of people 'reeling off the shopping list'. The UN agencies did want to break people's dependence on handouts, she explained, but it seemed there was still some way to go.

It was only the next day, back in Luanda, that we were able to put questions to De Mello, even if the press conference was late in starting. We waited on the veranda next to the pristine blue swimming pool at the new UN office. What was delaying De Mello's press conference, it turned out, was a meeting with aid workers who had presented him with a document suggesting that the UN's role in Angola had been 'helpful but not adequate in addressing human rights issues'. Rather diplomatically put. Yet once the press conference got going, it was De Mello himself who proved to be the consummate diplomat, deflecting questions in the best tradition of his calling.

I asked De Mello whether he intended investigating human rights in Cabinda. (This was not long after Tina had been raped and André had seen his daughters shot in that province.)

'If you want to transform the role of the UN here into an investigative one, we will go nowhere, particularly not in the immediate future.'

He spoke of 'partnership', of 'efforts to reform the institutions of this country, including the army, the police, the justice system'.

When I visited the UN Human Rights Division in Luanda a year later, they had a staff of three, none of whom ever visited the provinces.

❖

While waiting for De Mello to appear, one of the Angolan journalists had filled me in on the big news story that I had missed while on holiday the previous week. *Angolense*, one of the independent weeklies, had published a list of Angola's 50 richest people. It sounded like the kind of thing that would be a throwaway

Sunday feature in most countries, but in Angola it had created an uproar – possibly because the list was headed by Dos Santos, and most of the people on the list were high-ranking officials in the government or the ruling party.

The journalist told me how the MPLA had put out a statement saying that criticism of the millionaires was anti-patriotic. I shook my head, remembering the MPLA's socialist history: 'The workers' party ...'

He smiled. 'The workers' party has become the millionaires' party.'

The ripples from the 'case of the millionaires' continued for weeks afterwards. The minister of defence, Kundi Paihama, brought a criminal libel suit against the editor, and won, though other officials who attempted legal action were eventually unsuccessful. The newspaper that had caused all the fuss soon became a collector's item, wily street vendors selling it at 1 000 kwanzas a copy – at the then current exchange rate, about 15 dollars.

'Someone who has lost everything in the war starts civilian life like this, without any money – what is the government thinking?'

It was February 2003, exactly a year after Savimbi's death. At the Uamba quartering area in Uige province, it was clear that UNITA's men were going nowhere. Patrício was from Huambo and had been with UNITA for 20 years. Fifteen of those years had been spent in the forests of Uige, a long way from the wide horizons of his native Huambo. In the Uamba quartering area there remained little of the optimism that the soldiers there had displayed during my previous visit six months earlier.

'We have been here in the north too long,' Patrício continued. 'We want to go back to our areas of origin; we are waiting for the government to fulfil the promises it undertook. So far we have not received the kind of money that would enable us to leave here and go to our home areas.'

In the last few years of its existence as a fighting force, with sanctions slashing its diamond income and the FAA cutting off its supply lines, UNITA and its men had learnt to get by with very little. A year later, the 100 000-strong army was waiting for charity. It brought to mind a conversation I had the previous year with a *Luandense* working as a driver for the Red Cross, at a time when the quartering areas were still new. 'Those people have been in the bush all their lives,' he had said. 'They don't understand a market economy.'

So much for Savimbi having been paraded at the White House as a free market hero.

The Luena peace agreement had stipulated that the soldiers and their families would be home and gainfully employed as farmers, or in their chosen vocation, by October 2002. The most concrete promise was the payment of a US $ 100 demobilisation allowance and the provision of the packages of seeds, farming tools and household utensils collectively referred to as 'kits' – always known by this English word that stuck out like a spike in a Portuguese or Umbundu sentence. In the end, these kits proved as elusive as the phonetics. The soldiers' mistake was to believe the promises. How were they to know that Angolan political discourse always conveniently failed to distinguish between plans and action?

In November the previous year – the month after the supposed deadline – the social services ministry had summoned journalists to a room chilled to temperatures more suitable for storing fresh meat to hear its plans for the 'social and productive reintegration' of the former guerrillas. The event started two hours late, the air-conditioning all the while freezing the sweat left on our backs by the hot spring morning outside. Then a quartet of ministry officials took turns to read out the entire policy document, bullet point by bullet point, refusing to answer questions until they had finished. When the proposed employment strategies for UNITA got as far as '*criação de coelhos*' (raising rabbits) there seemed little point in enduring the aircon any longer.

My visit to Uamba gave a more realistic idea of how much exactly the ministry was capable of. The journey, with a WFP team, was quicker than it had been the previous year; a girder bridge now spanned the river where last year everything had been lugged across on the raft. But Uamba itself remained unchanged. The WFP staff set up camp in a sooty room of one of the derelict buildings that had constituted the old village. Two apparently destitute characters slept on the floor of another room of the same house, and spent their days writing down names and figures in a tattered exercise book. They asked the WFP people for a lift back to the city; when this proved impossible, they begged a ride with the armed forces. The two men were not refugees, but civil servants. The administration did not appear to have a car available for its functionaries to go and conduct its census of UNITA. Programmes for raising rabbits – or any other kind of livestock – seemed a long way away.

Patrício's case was not unusual. Four months after the October deadline for the soldiers' return home, only 500 people had left Uamba. At the same time, more people were arriving. They, however, were never going to figure in the statistics written down in the ministry officials' tattered exercise book. They were never going to figure because they were women. The still-promised assistance worked on the assumption that every man was a soldier and every soldier was a man. Women and minors, even if they had carried weapons, had no right to aid other than as dependants of a male soldier. But these newcomers had arrived alone, or carrying children.

'I came here to the quartering area to try and find my husband, the father of my children,' said Celita, holding a baby on her lap. 'But when I arrived here I heard that my husband had died in the war. My children have no father.'

Her husband had been a UNITA soldier in Negage in the same province until the FAA had recaptured the town in 1997. She had stayed behind with her three children after he went into the bush and was kept by 'a man from the FAA'. This 'man from the FAA' was the father of the child she was holding. Abandoned by him, and with the war now over, Celita went in search of her husband. She knew that UNITA soldiers who had been active in the area might have ended up in Uamba.

Only after walking 150 kilometres to find him did she learn that her husband was dead. She had, by chance, learnt that her uncle, also a UNITA soldier, was in the camp. She now lived in his house, waiting, as everyone else in Uamba was waiting, for the promised help that might get her back to Huambo.

Adriana also had a story to tell. She too had been in Negage when her husband 'went to the bush' with UNITA.

'The police raped me, and as a result of this I became pregnant. I left there because I was abandoned, and came here to look for my husband.'

Adriana, at least, was reunited with her husband in the gathering area: as close to a happy ending as such a story might have.

To talk to Celita and Adriana I had first to seek the permission of the relevant UNITA official: in this case, a woman called Jorgina who was in charge of women's welfare. She was coldly confident that the women would recover from their trauma.

'Rape by police or the army, this was something that happened in time of war,' she said. 'This phase is now past. Even those husbands whose wives have been raped are coming to terms with this and will stay with them.'

Colonel Elíseu, the deputy commandant of the Uamba camp, was a man with a concentrated stare who never smiled with his mouth, but sometimes seemed to with his eyes; it was hard not to see this as sardonic. His shirt was bright scarlet, and it suited him. His office was another of the empty rooms of Uamba's abandoned village. There was a charcoal drawing on the wall, the caption 'UNITA 1999' indicating that it dated from an earlier period of occupation: the drawing showed a storybook palace, like a child's building-block fantasy, with turrets and spires. A flag flew over the building, the emblem on the flag a kind of squashed duck, which I took to be UNITA's *galo negro* (black cockerel) emblem.

The colonel talked to me about the women coming back to look for their husbands. What if a woman came back with a child fathered by someone from the other side, would they welcome her, I asked.

He gave me that non-smile.

'To accept a woman who is carrying another man's child – that's all part of national reconciliation.'

Here at Uamba, on UNITA soil – albeit circumscribed by the government and under the supervision of Jorgina – all the women spoke of the UNITA men as their real husbands, and those from the other side as rapists or, at best, as 'a man who kept me'. It was hard not to think that if I had interviewed these same women in Negage and under MPLA rule, the stories would have been phrased differently. Back in Luanda, I spoke to Mary Daly, an Irish doctor who had spent more than 20 years in Angola. She confirmed this suspicion: 'Where the military determine who has food and who hasn't, and they are the people who determine who has access to a number of things, women use the only thing they have which is of value, which is themselves and their bodies,' she said. 'I have seen it happen with the acquiescence of the entire family. They describe the political aspects of it differently, but the real aspects of force are the same.'

A small number of UNITA's soldiers had managed to leave the quartering areas, but they had not got very far. Some of them were regretting having left at all. At the edge of Uige city, just before the *bairros* dissolved into countryside, was Kituma, a collection of neat, rectangular mud-brick houses strung out across the green hillside.

'When I arrived here I understood that in terms of the peace accord this was a transit area, and within two or three days I would be able to move on to my home area,' said Costa, a soldier who had left a quartering area in Zaire province, and was waiting to get home to Maquela do Zombo, in the north of Uige province. He had already been there for more than two months – further from home now than he had been in the quartering area.

'People left behind the vegetable gardens and maize fields they had been cultivating in the quartering areas,' complained Gabriel, another ex-UNITA soldier. 'We don't have that here in the city.'

The transit centres were among the weakest of the many links in the government's plans to get all the UNITA soldiers home. The FAA's lumbering trucks would bring people from the quartering areas to the nearest provincial transit centre; there, they would assemble with others from the same home area and, in theory, be trucked home; or, if home was beyond the range of the trucks, they would be taken to the nearest airport and loaded onto the Russian planes. In fact, as Costa and Gabriel had discovered, the plan seldom went as smoothly as that.

Kituma had been built during the war as a resettlement centre for people displaced by the fighting, many of whom would have been MPLA supporters who had fled under attack from UNITA. A good number of these people were still at Kituma to see the arrival of their new neighbours: the members of the very same army that they had come here to get away from. This was exactly the kind of situation that Simão, the man I had spoken to in Kuito the previous year, had feared when he made his sceptical predictions about how far reconciliation could go.

I asked Samuel, one of the civilians who had been in Kituma since 1997, whether his past experience of UNITA had not soured his opinions of the new arrivals. He replied: 'We who were on the side of the government were attacked by our colleagues who are now here together with us.'

One of the aid staff put it another way: 'They all get on well, because they are all so angry with the government.'

Reconciliation in Angola took on some unusual forms.

Later I talked to a fierce-looking teenager in a red singlet and flat-top haircut, who softened as we spoke.

'I was captured by UNITA when I was a child.'

It was only six months since I had spoken to the boys of Uamba who thought there was nothing wrong with kidnapping children. Loyalties were starting to unravel. It was now possible to admit that one's own abduction was not a good thing.

UNITA's leadership in Luanda were having more success reintegrating than their foot soldiers in the provinces. The political committee had found a new office next door to the Brandãos' house, where I had filed my reports about UNITA kidnapping children in Caxito and attacking the city of Uige shortly after I arrived in Luanda for the first time. They no longer had to do business in the Trópico lounge.

One Saturday morning I ran into Anabela in a supermarket, and she invited me to come and visit. 'We're still there, in spite of what the papers say.' She had been furious when one of the independent weeklies had wrongly reported that her house, rather than the neighbour's, had been sold to UNITA. In fact, the woman who had sold her house to the former rebels was the widow of an FAA brigadier.

Joffre Justino had moved back to Luanda, and sending UNITA press releases was no longer his responsibility. But he had kept his e-mailing list, and I now received from him advertisements for herbal health products, and at Easter an e-card with a pink animated Easter Bunny. This, it appeared, was as close to *criação de coelhos* as UNITA was ever going to get.

The government's attention was elsewhere. In February 2002, Angola took up a non-permanent seat on the UN Security Council, at a time when the council was facing one of its deepest divisions in years. Those attacks on the far shore of the Atlantic Ocean nearly 18 months earlier, which had been discussed with such fascinated detachment by the people of downtown Luanda, had been the cue for a new mood in American foreign policy, whose consequences we were now seeing in President Bush's determination to go to war against Iraq.

As an oil-producing country with a Muslim population close to zero, Angola was never likely to escape the State Department's attention. A stately new American embassy, intended as a pastiche of Portuguese colonial architecture, was starting to rise on the site of the trailer park that had hitherto served as the US mission. But now, with every Security Council vote expected to count one way or the other when it came to Washington's plans for a certain other oil-producing country, the courting of Angola became more important than ever.

Under-Secretary of State Walter Kannsteiner paid a brief visit. Lounging in the squishy brown leather armchairs of the airport's protocol section, he did a passable impersonation of someone who had just dropped in for a quiet chat.

'I'm in Africa on a trip into the region and so I thought it would be opportune to take this chance to come to Luanda and discuss a number of international and bilateral issues with the president,' he replied when asked about the purpose of his visit.

Was the question of Angola's support for military action against Iraq on the agenda for his talks with Dos Santos, I ventured.

'We did discuss international issues including issues that are in front of the Security Council right now – that would include Iraq and Côte d'Ivoire and a number of other issues. We discussed what has been presented to the Security Council on Iraq, and future discussions are pending.'

A week later, he was followed by Baroness Valerie Amos, who was then the British Foreign Office minister responsible for Africa.

'We're just setting out our position,' she insisted, a touch impatiently, standing amid a clump of journalists on her way to the boarding gate. 'Our concern about the violation of Security Council resolutions over 12 years, Saddam Hussein's determination to have weapons of mass destruction and the fact that this is undermining the credibility of the UN.'

Next came the French foreign minister, Dominique de Villepin, as though Paris were trying to trump its Anglophone rivals by sending a more senior official. By this time, the Angolan government was loving the attention. It did not seem to matter too much that foreign minister João de Miranda could not make it to the airport to welcome his French counterpart. Instead, he waited for De Villepin in the air-conditioned baroque of the presidential palace, chatting to the journalists with an affability unbecoming an Angolan government official. He greeted *'Monsieur le ministre'*, apologising for not having been present at the airport. But the symbolism was clear enough: Like Kannsteiner and Amos before him, De Villepin had come looking for a favour.

It was hard to begrudge Miranda his delight. The Angolan government had spent 15 years as a pawn of the superpowers during the Cold War, and a further decade watching one diplomatic blueprint after another fail to bring peace to the country. Now, suddenly, it had a chance to say yes or no to a war that already looked set to become a defining moment in international relations for the decade and beyond.

After Miranda and De Villepin emerged from the inner room where President Dos Santos granted audiences, the Angolan minister seemed determined to prolong the moment, making it clear to the journalists that Angola was not going to commit itself one way or the other until it came to the Security Council vote.

'There has been talk of pressure, but we do not feel that pressure – we are discussing with all partners on the Security Council in order to be able to reach the most viable and most justifiable solution possible. The Angolan position is closer neither to the US nor to France – it is Angola's position.'

His declaration of neutrality did not stop Baroness Amos coming back for another crack, saying that Britain was proposing a new resolution that might be more acceptable to the wavering Security Council members. But by now there was speculation that France would use the power of veto that it held as a permanent member of the council, rendering irrelevant the opinions of Angola and the other non-permanent member states.

In the end, France never had the chance to exercise its veto since the war began without a further Security Council vote. If the Angolan government had come to a decision on which way to vote, that decision was never made known. The question became increasingly academic as British and American troops approached Baghdad – and Angola's rulers unblinkingly contradicted each other on the subject.

When the Angolan parliament convened to debate the war, one by one, members from the MPLA, from UNITA and from the little opposition parties stood up stiffly and read out their pre-prepared condemnations of the invasion of Iraq. At the end, the deputy foreign minister, Jorge Chicoty, said the government shared the opinion that had been expressed unanimously by the parliamentarians. Later that week, the US ambassador, Chris Dell, told an Angolan radio interviewer that João de Miranda had communicated to Colin Powell Angola's support for the American position on the Iraq question.

From Joffre Justino came an e-mail requesting recipients to show their opposition to the war by means of a candle in a window. This arrived at a time when I was lighting candles most nights, war or no war. Luanda's colonial-era power grid could never keep up with the demands of summer air-conditioning, and electricity cuts were more frequent now than ever before.

Life went on, however, as ever. Across the road from my flat, an elderly Portuguese couple ran a business that stubbornly disregarded the era of the supermarket, the tinned food and the cleaning products stacked behind the counter, the towels and bed linen folded on shelves. The wine, all of it Portuguese, stayed in a high glass-fronted cabinet. The owners or their staff would calculate the bill by hand on a piece of white wrapping paper.

Senhor was always glad of the chance to talk about the war with a journalist, though, since he had a satellite dish, he was usually more up to date on events in Iraq than I was. 'Those palaces,' he recounted one morning after CNN had followed American soldiers into one of Saddam Hussein's residences. 'All those treasures, in a country where people are starving ...'

'Yes, just the same as here,' I replied.

The couple looked at me with delighted horror. 'You mustn't say that,' they implored in conspiratorial stage whispers.

For Holden Roberto, meanwhile, the war on Iraq signalled the downfall of the American empire.

'Who destroyed the Roman Empire? It destroyed itself. Those Americans can't be soldiers. I once went to the Vietnam War memorial in Washington. There were men, soldiers, weeping. How can you fight a war like that?'

As an American protégé who had been dropped when the going got tough, he spoke perhaps with some authority.

❖

On the day that America and Britain defied the United Nations and started bombing Iraq, the UN mission in Angola issued a press release: 'The UN has declared 2003 International Fresh Water Year. To mark the launch of the event, and to coincide with the Third

Global Forum on Water, to take place in the Japanese city of Kyoto from 16 to 23 of this month, we attach four official documents on the subject, for publication.'

On the global stage, now, the UN had been pushed aside, just as the international body had been left as nothing more than a spectator to events in Angola a year earlier, when the strapping FAA officers had presented their plan for peace to the frail UNITA men in Luena. The UN humanitarian agencies were still there, though, and UNICEF had put up the money for a measles vaccination campaign in Angola. The agency's chief executive, Carol Bellamy, visited Luanda, for the launch in Cassenga, a *bairro* just far enough from the city to look suitably poverty-stricken, but not so far that the important guests would have to spend more than half an hour getting there. Red and white balloons, the campaign colours, decorated the school chosen for the launch; the banners and T-shirts displayed the same colours. Along the rutted street outside, children from other schools were lined up for vaccination. And the MPLA youth were there with their megaphones, making sure that the vaccination queue became a welcoming party for the president and first lady.

Dos Santos, amigo
O povo está contigo!

When the presidential couple arrived, they were displaying their support by wearing the red and white campaign T-shirts. In keeping with the colour scheme, first lady Ana Paula dos Santos was wearing diamond and ruby earrings.

Seventy-two year old Pricila Nakangwe was learning to read for the first time, in her village of Santa Teresa on the outskirts of Huambo city. ('When I was at school, we only learnt to copy Bible verses,' she explained.) Outside, the first rains had cleared the Planalto air of its winter dust; the mielies were already growing tall, while women hoed the rust-coloured earth to carry on planting. Mud bricks dried in the sun.

It was October 2003 and, in the 18 months since the peace accord, some people at least had managed to go home. Santa Teresa was growing. The adult education classes that Pricila was attending, organised by a donor agency, were open to all, but most of the learners were demobilised soldiers.

One of old Pricila's classmates, 37-year-old Domingos Silva, had been conscripted into the Angolan Army at age 15 and had spent more than 20 years in the forces before being demobilised. Now he had come home and was learning to read. He seemed unperturbed by the fact that former UNITA soldiers were coming home to the same village.

'In these days of peace, we're working together, MPLA and UNITA. There's no conflict at all.'

But if there was no conflict, it seemed this had a lot to do with the fact that the UNITA people kept themselves to themselves in the village.

Sebastião Tavares, aged 21, had been a soldier with UNITA from the age of 16. Now he sat on the steps of the mud-brick church building with two friends, both of them former UNITA soldiers too. Sebastião was born in Lubango. But by the end of the war he knew of no relatives surviving there, so he had decided to go to Huambo, 'my mother's land'. He may well have had a maternal connection with the province. But it was hardly a coincidence that, in the absence of living relatives, he had gone to a place where he would at least be in the company of some former comrades.

The soldiers themselves were full of talk of reconciliation, of moving on – of being sons of the area, brothers who had had no choice over which army had conscripted them. It was the aid workers, the ones who could afford to take a longer view, who, like Simão in Kuito, dared to sound caution.

Four years earlier, Santa Teresa had been on the front line. Elíseu, one of the organisers of the literacy classes, indicated the mountains that seemed barely an arm's length away in that clear air: 'Until 1999, those mountains were controlled by UNITA.'

'People don't know about consensus,' Elíseu continued. 'For a long time, they have been seeing people fighting, dying. It's not easy to change within one year what you have learnt over 30 years.'

❖

At the end of 2003, the MPLA held its Fifth Congress, the first such congress since the war. Entering his 25th year in office, President José Eduardo dos Santos was re-elected as party chairman. No other candidates had put their names forward for the party leadership.

❖

Angola comes to an end at Luau, halting abruptly at a bridge over the River Cassai that forms the border between Moxico province and the Democratic Republic of Congo. The border post on the railway that once connected Benguela and Lobito with the Congo and Zambia is located at Luau.

A mere two blocks from the park that marks the civic centre, I reached the edge of town, crossing the road into a forest of grass higher than my head. Further on, in a clearing were steam locomotives, still with their brass plaques identifying them as having been built in Glasgow in 1930.

The locomotives were long dead. But cellphones worked, which seemed strange given the paucity of network coverage in the Angolan interior. The cellphones of Luau came from a market in the Democratic Republic of Congo and picked up their signal from a mast across the border. To reach Luanda meant an international call. Although it provided a signal, however, the Congo could not provide electricity, and the local delegate of the Angolan Red Cross would regularly visit the office of the United Nations High Commissioner for Refugees (UNHCR) to charge up his phone battery during the hours when the generator was switched on.

The UNHCR had set up a base in Luau because, during the course of the war, some 200 000 people had left Angola for the Democratic Republic of Congo, or Zaire as it was then known. A similar number were in Zambia. The UNHCR had built a compound, a thatch-grass simulacrum of military barracks, for those who would start making their way across the bridge as soon as the agency launched its repatriation programme at the beginning of June.

Some had walked back already. If Luau was the end of Angola to an eastbound traveller, it ought to have been the beginning of Angola for someone coming west. Yet Luau's Bairro Jika and Bairro

Progresso looked more like a dead end. In Jika, on the edge of the town, people were living in a minefield. The red-painted stakes that the de-mining organisations habitually placed as a warning around mined areas here took on the aspect of suburban picket fences – with the adobe houses on the inside. The de-miners, Angolans employed by a British NGO, showed us the morning's find: an anti-personnel device the size of a saucer.

'People are difficult,' the leader of the de-mining team explained, exasperated that the residents had chosen to construct their homes in that particular spot. 'They had previously always lived in that *bairro*. They arrived there to settle during the night.'

In fact, there was nowhere else to go. The roads from Luau had been closed to traffic throughout the rainy season. There was a way in, over the bridge from the Congo, but no way out. Luau's surplus people were overflowing, even into the minefields.

Bairro Progresso, meanwhile, could not have been more wrongly named. For a start, an hour's walk out of Luau, it was hardly a *bairro*, in the sense of being organically linked to a city. On the other hand, it did not have the subsistence fields that would have made it a properly rural village. And progress was in short supply. Among its residents were several *desmobilizados* from Calala – that other place on Angola's eastern limb, the quartering area with the traffic roundabout and the surgeon in his gown, where I had met Adriano Keto, the son of the policeman from Luanda, and all those other soldiers who had seen in the future a peace that would be crafted in the same clockwork dependability that they had learnt to expect in Savimbi's army.

That was not the way it had turned out.

The men had not been well received by the local population. They survived by '*troco de força*' (exchange of force, of effort), a phrase with a ring to it of the phrase '*troco de fogo*' – exchange of fire. They worked for 'the people who have fields – those who stayed here, or who came back from the Congo'. They received *bombó*: manioc tubers. No cash.

'Many of us have professions, but we have nowhere to go. We are ready to go back to Huambo and Bié. But we have no money, no work,' they explained. Nor did they have any notion of what it meant to live in the multi-party democracy that Angola – in theory – had been since 1992.

'We know we are with the government because the government brought us here,' said a man named João Baptista. 'But then other people say we are from UNITA. No one takes responsibility for us.'

I thought now not of the hopeful men of Calala, but of Mavinga, of the woman who had spoken smilingly of how her affiliations had changed as she crossed the line of control from one army to the other.

'Are you still a member of UNITA?'

'No, now I'm a member of the government.'

'What makes you a member of the government?'

'Because I am here with the government.'

Nearly two years on, in Bairro Progresso, the vision persisted not of one Angola in which political choices might be made, but of two unequal and conflicted Angolas, of which only one, the victor, had the capacity to provide. Some people, however, had not been able to switch sides as easily as the woman in Mavinga.

In the government social services office – a crumbling building equipped with a few tables and chairs – an official showed us the boxes of completed repatriation forms which UNHCR had handed out on the understanding that the completed forms would entitle the holder to the issuance of an Angolan national identity card. Proudly showing his guests how much paperwork the office had managed to gather, he pulled a form off the top of the pile and offered it as a souvenir: 'You can keep it.'

'The so-called colonist of today is worse than the previous one.'

In Luena, some 500 kilometres from Luau, Dom Gabriel Mbilingue, Bishop of Moxico, believed he was one of the few people in the province who could talk of the MPLA in this way without fear of reprisal.

'The government says it is reintegrating the ex-combatants in a dignified manner – but it's not helping in our province. The help is being done by the Salesians. The Luena agreement is not functioning.'

The reception centre run by the Salesian fathers was on the opposite side of Luena from the bishop's house, in one of the half-derelict warehouse buildings near the old railway. Where the road crossed the railway tracks, there were shiny new signs with a locomotive icon warning drivers of the presence of the railway. Trains did not appear to be a clear and present danger; the remaining wagons still appeared fused to the tracks as they had for the past two years, and the only locomotives in Moxico province were the dead ones in Luau.

I approached some men loitering outside the warehouse to find out whether they were staff or residents of the centre.

'We are visitors,' they said, in English.

All of them were Angolans bewildered in their own country, recently back from Zambia and waiting to go to homes that they were not sure they would recognise. Like 32-year-old Tito who had lived since he was ten years of age in Zambia under the name of Titus, most of them knew no Portuguese and had little hope of finding a job.

Judith, who was there with her six children, had crossed the border at Cazombo.

Why had she come to Luena?

'I don't know. I wanted to go to Lumbala Nguimbo, but they put us on a plane to Luena.'

Three weeks later, Judith and her children were still sleeping on the concrete warehouse floor.

On the road leading out of Luena, there was no roadblock, but straggling partygoers were enough to make the driver slow down. Two half-drunk girls swayed their hips behind an MPLA flag that they were holding between them at waist height. The road ahead was sprinkled with pieces of brown beer-bottle glass in between the potholes. The road to Muacanheca was also the road to a lake, which was referred to in Luena only half ironically as '*a praia*' – the beach – which seemed to be the place to go to get out of town on a Sunday.

Muacanheca was the camp that had been thrown together around the time Savimbi had died to accommodate the thousands whom the FAA had driven out of the *mata* and into the towns; it was the camp where, two years ago, I had spoken to young Graça and weary Eduardo shortly after they had stumbled into government territory.

Two years on, the city of blue tarpaulins was no more and Muacanheca had condensed into a collection of adobe houses under the mango trees by the roadside. It looked like a village now. There were dogs. The aid agencies had left, and the health post they had established now had no medicine and offered no jobs.

'Children are dying from the lack of doctors,' said the *bairro* secretary, a man called Antunes. 'Many people decided to go back to their *terras*, without getting help from anyone.'

Those who, like Antunes, came from further away, had no chance of getting home on foot and were surviving as best they could.

'The people are at the end of their tether. There are widows who start at two in the morning to walk to the city and sell charcoal. Recently the *fiscais* started working inside the city, without any reason. Now only those who have an identity document can go to town and sell. And no one has an identity document.'

It was easy to imagine the application forms for those documents lying in an office like the one in Luau, and maybe being offered as a souvenir to a curious visitor. More than just the right to sell charcoal, those cards were what would entitle people to vote once the government called the elections, more than six years overdue.

I wondered if the people of Muacanheca felt they were being discriminated against.

'If you want to ask if there is discrimination, this is up to the government.'

As we talked, a truck rumbled by as fast as the fractured road surface would allow. The noise of the engine itself might not have been enough to drown our conversation, but the yelling and chanting from the people packed onto the back of the lorry –

many of them in the scarlet T-shirts of the MPLA Youth – certainly did.

A thousand kilometres from the sea, the victors were going to the beach.

June 2001. Kuito, eight years after the siege of 1993.

December 2001. A strange calm in Luena, capital of Moxico, where Jonas Savimbi hid out at the end of the war.

June 2002. Cuemba, with trade still in the hands of those with access to air transport.

June 2002. Carlos, 15, (centre), in Cuemba at the end of the war after two years of active service.

July 2002. Mavinga, 'at the end of the earth', after successive battles between the government and UNITA.

September 2002. At the end of the war, António Domingos, 15, reunited with his mother, Paulina, three years after UNITA attacked Malange.

Bibliography

Bender, Gerald. *Angola Under the Portuguese.* Africa World Press, Trenton, 2004.

Bridgland, Fred. *Jonas Savimbi: A Key to Africa.* Macmillan South Africa, Johannesburg, 1986.

Brittain, Victoria. *Death of Dignity: Angola's Civil War.* Pluto, London, 1998.

Chabal, Patrick. *A History of Postcolonial Lusophone Africa.* Hurst, London, 2002.

Chabal, Patrick, and Jean-Pascal Daloz. *Africa Works: Disorder as a Political Instrument.* James Currey, Oxford, 1999.

Cilliers, Jackie and Christian Dietrich (eds). *Angola's War Economy: The Role of Oil and Diamonds.* Institute for Security Studies, Pretoria, 2000.

Coppé, Margrit and Fergus Power (eds). *Stories for Trees: Stories and Images of Angola.* Development Workshop, Luanda, 2002.

Davidson, Basil. *In the Eye of the Storm: Angola's People.* Longman, London, 1972.

Guimarães, Fernando Andresen. *The Origins of the Angolan Civil War: Foreign Intervention and Domestic Political Conflict.* Macmillan, London, 2001.

Hammann, Hilton. *Days of the Generals.* Zebra, Cape Town, 2001.

Hart, Keith and Joanna Lewis (eds). *Why Angola Matters.* African Studies Centre, Cambridge, 1994.

Hodges, Tony. *Angola: Anatomy of an Oil State.* James Currey, Oxford, 2003.

Human Rights Watch. *Angola Unravels: The Rise and Fall of the Lusaka Peace Process.* Human Rights Watch, New York, 1999.

Human Rights Watch. *Unfinished Democracy: Media and political freedoms in Angola.* Human Rights Watch, New York, 2004.

Human Rights Watch. *Angola: Between war and peace in Cabinda.* Human Rights Watch. New York, 2004.

Human Rights Watch. *Going Home: Return and Resettlement in Angola.* Human Rights Watch, New York, 2005.

Kapuscinski, Ryszard. *Another Day of Life.* Penguin, London, 2001.

Maier, Karl. *Angola: Promises and Lies.* Serif, London, 1996.

Marques, Rafael and Rui Falcão de Campos (eds). *Angola's Deadly Diamonds: Human Rights Abuses in the Lunda Provinces.* Unpublished paper, 2005.

Matloff, Judith. *Fragments of a Forgotten War.* Penguin Books (South Africa), Johannesburg, 1997.

Meijer, Guus. *From Military Peace to Social Justice? The Angolan Peace Process.* Issue 15 of *Accord*, Conciliation Resources, London, 2004.

Pearce, Justin. *War, peace and diamonds in Angola: Popular perceptions of the diamond industry in the Lundas.* Institute for Security Studies, Pretoria, 2004.

Steenkamp, Willem. *Adeus Angola.* Howard Timmins, Cape Town, 1976.

Stockwell, John. *In Search of Enemies: A CIA Story.* Deutsch, London, 1978.

Index